ino Campana **Orphic Songs**
Translated by I. L. Salomon
Pocket Poets Series Number 54

CITY LIGHTS BOOKS
San Francisco

ORPHIC SONGS

Dino Campana Opere © 1989 by Editori Associate, S.p.A., Milano
English translation © 1968 by I. L. Salomon
First City Lights edition 1998
All Rights Reserved
10 9 8 7 6 5 4 3 2 1

Cover Design: Rex Ray
Book Design: Nancy J. Peters
Typography: Harvest Graphics

Library of Congress Cataloging-in-Publication Data

Campana, Dino, 1885-1932.
     [Canti orfici. English & Italian]
     Orphic songs / Dino Campana ; translated I.L. Salomon.
        p.   cm. — (Pocket poets series ; no. 54)
     ISBN 0-87286-340-9
     I. Salomon, Isidore Lawrence, 1899-   . II. Title.
PQ4809.A52C313   1988
851'.912—dc21   98-9893
                                                                  CIP

City Lights Books are available to bookstores through our
primary distributor: Subterranean Company. P. O. Box 160,
265 S. 5th St., Monroe, OR 97456. 541-847-5274. Toll-free
orders 800-274-7826. FAX 541-847-6018. Our books are also
available through library jobbers and regional distributors. For
personal orders and catalogs, please write to City Lights Books,
261 Columbus Avenue, San Francisco, CA 94133, or visit our
Web site: http//www.citylights.com

CITY LIGHTS BOOKS are edited by Lawrence Ferlinghetti and
Nancy J. Peters and published at the City Lights Bookstore,
261 Columbus Avenue, San Francisco, CA 94133.

For Milton and Paul

CONTENTS

ACKNOWLEDGMENTS

My thanks to the editors of the following periodicals in printing a number of these poems, a few in earlier versions: *Poetry Northwest, The Minnesota Review, Tri-Quarterly, Commonweal, Il Giornalino* and *Forum Italicum,* and my immeasurable gratitude to the National Council on the Arts for giving me complete freedom to work.

For reading the final draft of these translations and making extremely pertinent suggestions, I owe a great debt to Sergio Baldi and the poet Alfredo de Palchi. The following scholars, translators and poets had their part in setting me right when I faltered in my Italian and I am grateful for their generous help: Glauco Cambon, Michael Campo, Giuseppe Cardillo, Maria Di Sevo, Maria Gargotta, Giuliano Innamorati, poet Mario Luzi, Iole Magri, Marco Miele, Olga Ragusa, poet Silvio Ramat, Zina Tillona, and Joseph Tusiani. In writing the introduction and notes, I have used the following publications freely and I wish to thank the authors, editors, publishers: Carlo Betocchi. "Dino Campana, Vita e Poesia" (*Il Veltro,* Dec. 1957); Piero Bigongiari. *Poesia italiana del novecento* (Vallecchi, 1965); Giovanni Bonalumi. *Cultura e Poesia di Campana* (Vallecchi, 1953); Neuro Bonifazi. *Dino Campana* (Edizioni dell'Ateneo, 1964); Campana-Aleramo. *Lettere* (Vallecchi, 1958); Dino Campana. *Canti Orfici e altri scritti* (Vallecchi, 1962); Dino Campana. *Taccuinetto Faentino* (Vallecchi, 1960); Enrico Falqui. *Per una cronistoria dei "Canti*

Orfici" (Vallecchi, 1960); Gino Gerola. *Dino Campana* (Sansoni, 1955); Maria Serafina Mazza, S.C. *Not for Art's Sake* (King's Crown Press, 1948); Carlo Pariani. *Vite, non romanzate di Dino Campana scrittore e di Evaristo Boncinelli scultore* (Vallecchi, 1938); Silvio Ramat. *Campana, Canti Orfici* (Economica Vallecchi, 1966); Jean-Arthur Rimbaud. *Oeuvres Complètes* (Brentano's, undated).

These translations are dedicated to H. Lawrence Helfer, Sergio Baldi, Charles Schuman, M.D., and Fraser Bragg Drew.

INTRODUCTION

After Dante, or better, together with Dante, Dino Campana (1885–1932) is the most international of Italian poets. If there is a characteristic of Campana's that from the beginning distinguished him, it is his *inadmissibility* in his own time and world, both in his life and in his poetry.

Campana, like Rimbaud, Whitman, Dylan Thomas, created neither a school nor a tradition. His poetry and his career were destined to remain solitary. All in all, in the literary world he was tolerated rather than loved. Campana is in fact unclassifiable, unlabelable, unhistoricizable, according to the canons and conventions by which poetry is generally judged.

The poetic experience and the figure of Campana—fragmented, unmistakably unbreakable, broke too violently the ordered picture of nineteenth-century Italian poetry, by definition centered on three founders—Saba, Ungaretti, and Montale. Great poets, certainly, but compared to Campana they appear as but the best bearers of the classical national tradition, of poetic experience limited by Italian borders, whereas the immediate reference for Dino Campana is European (Nietzsche, Rimbaud, Baudelaire) and international (Whitman, Poe).

Thus D'Annunzio used Nietzsche, taking however only his ideological point of view, whereas Campana absorbed his deeper substance, transcending the rational horizon to reveal a new world of freer and more fertile imagination,

mediated by the burning vision that consumed him, by the uniqueness of his poetic and existential exploration.

"I want to create a musical, colored, European poetry. I have brought a sense of color that didn't exist before in Italian poetry" : colors, lights, shades of darkness and sudden illuminations, a world at the same time in full sun and twilight, auroral and nocturnal, made of boundless seascapes, impenetrable mountains, turreted cities isolated in eternal silences. And then the travel, the trips and the returns, the partings and re-partings in known and unknown alternation, which perhaps embodied the deepest metaphor of his poetry: constant oscillation, life as oscillation and perpetual balancing between "vision" and so-called "reality."

In this eternal oscillation, Campana's poetry attains a precarious and incredible equilibrium, perfectly reproduced and expiated in the skin of his existence, and not in any case to be called "mental disequilibrium"—a unique and rare condition, isolated and mysterious fruit of the spirit transcending national boundaries of whatever type: "total" poetry that embraces the entire world and speaks to all as a "new language," a seering vision that sees all that man and the normal poet don't risk discerning.

It's too easy to count Campana among the "poètes maudits" although his biography, like Rimbaud's, is their exact stereotype. His "madness" places him close to Nietzsche and Artaud. And his poetry, which is also prose and comes close to Baudelaire's "little poems in prose," seems the very emblem of Rimbaud's cherished "illuminations." But it's possible to

place Campana in a larger genre, a category that includes "poètes maudits" but also all those who remain "nomads"— all those involved in Futurism, Symbolism, Orphism, Surrealism, hermeticism.

Everything burns and melds in his writing and in his life, like a whole that is more than the sum of its parts. A restlessness, a not knowing how to settle in a single place, a disequilibrium that we find only in other great meteors of poetry and literature: Poe, Dylan Thomas, Rimbaud, Kerouac, Artaud . . . a nomadism on an existential level— Switzerland, France, Argentina, and the long interminable routes of the Apennines . . . and then Faenza, Turin, Marradi, Geneva, Florence, Bologna, Genoa, Buenos Aires, Nizza, Forli . . . and the brawls, the forced labor, the most desperate trades, the most far-out loves, the madhouse. And poetry always, poetry above all, with all, a lacerating force and an opening onto new skies summed up in every moment of his life: "I don't live, I exist in a state of continual suggestion, I'm hypnotic to a high degree, I'm full of magnetic currents . . . ."

He who was not serene now reposes at Badia a Settimo on the outskirts of Florence, under a slab of serene stone: "And I will travel on a flying carpet, red and moving, like a king in exile, in a dream of a kingdom above the skies."

Antonio Bertoli
Firenze, 1997

Tr: L. Ferlinghetti

TRANSLATOR'S PREFACE

Dino Campana was the wild man of Italian poetry in 1914, on the eve of the Great War. He is as important to 20th-century poetry as, say, Lorca or Mayakovsky. His poems and prose poems are unique. They read as if they were thrown into the wind in an ecstasy of violence. They reflect the disintegration of a man.

Campana has been compared to Rimbaud. His *Orphic Songs* lacks the cohesiveness of the poems in *The Drunken Boat* or the prose poems in *The Illuminations*. There are affinities: fantastic fervor, a fine frenzy of poetic image, metaphors in transfiguration. In their lives there are only surface resemblances: each rebelled against the provincialism of his upbringing. At odds with the world, each was more at odds with himself. In search of answers to imponderables, each roamed the cities of the world.

A university dropout, Campana discovered the poetry of Walt Whitman. In *Leaves of Grass* the intense individualism, extravagant rhetoric, and democratic humanity overwhelmed him. In homage to Whitman, Campana closed *Orphic Songs* with a quotation faultily remembered. Every edition since concludes with this line from "Song of Myself": *They were all torn and cover'd with the boy's blood.*

Whitman celebrates the common man, rampant as grass among the leaves in a land green with promise. Campana hungered for this freedom from old-world restraint. In

Whitman the body, flesh and spirit of man are worshiped as holy; there is nothing evil, all is sacred. In Campana these elements of man's being burn in a purgatory of purification. This is the fulfillment of Goethe's "Stirb und werde," a holy longing to "Die and become"—a modern philosophic variation on an Orphic myth.

In rebellion against the bourgeoisie and in his desire to embrace "pure idealism," Campana dedicated *Orphic Songs* to Kaiser Wilhelm II in 1914. Although he subtitled his book "The Last German in Italy," he recognized the seeds of subversion and destruction in Nietzsche and in Wagner. Not too long after, he disclaimed his dedication in "Franco-Italian Proletarian Song": *Italy/I love you with immeasurable aching.* Campana spent the last fourteen years of his life in Castel Pulci, The Psychiatric Hospital, near Florence.

Marradi, where Dino Campana was born, is a mountain township encrusted in the Apennines. This is rugged, forbidding country. Geographically, it lies in Romagna, where Tuscan speech has not deprived the natives of their dialect. Politically, it is in the province of Florence.

The forty mile drive from Florence northeast to Marradi is not easy. The climb to the mountain gap, 3000 feet above sea level, is steep. The descent through the Val di Lamone, the heart of the valley, is breathtaking. Like a snake the road coils through the countryside, its flanks, strata of rock on strata. On the mountains there are cypress, cedar, poplar; on the lower slope, thick foliage; below this, small groves. The road follows the running stream into Marradi.

Here, Dino spent a "happy" childhood, slightly repressed by the severe discipline of his parents. His father, Giovanni, principal of the elementary school, was a martinet, an ardent patriot, a forthright member of the community; his mother, Fanny Luti of a well-to-do family, was an eccentric who kept aloof from her neighbors. She used to wander up into the hills, fingering her rosary, frequently forgetting to prepare dinner for her husband and children, Dino and the younger Manlio. As she moved among the rocks, was she a younger Gioconda her son was to write of? Or "The Octopus of Mediterranean nights" in Genoa, bearing within her secrets best hidden in the grave? Or Ophelia under the red street-lamps in Bologna? Or the Little Madonna of the Bridge, transfigured in her niche on the stone wall in Marradi?

In Campana's poetry, women are the pitiless devourers of men, their willing victims. There is conflict here between the natural desire for sex and its moral prohibition. He was fifteen when his world collapsed at this confrontation. He became intemperate, brutal, abusive, morbid. His savage resentment against his mother sent him to an asylum. Under medical treatment there and forbearance at home, he recovered from his first attack.

Like all Italian boys preparing for the university, Dino studied the ancient tongues, Latin and Greek. He had a good ear for the modern languages and was quite fluent in French, German, and English. Unaware that his steps were directed by his father, he listened to the advice of the local pharmacist, Ciottoli, and enrolled under the Faculty of

Chemistry at the University of Bologna. His volatility, inexperience, and unwillingness to adapt himself to the mores of the herd set him apart. In the laboratory, he worked more like an alchemist than an objective scientist. His desire to encompass all knowledge led him to German metaphysics, French and Spanish poetry, and to the esoteric doctrines of the Orphic mysteries. He discovered in them an Orpheus, his miraculous song submerged, returned from the world of the dead, a Redeemer figure of a new mystical religion. In this pagan fountain he steeped his distraught desires. If Orphism, twenty-five centuries old, bound him, Walt Whitman as prophet and poet, making a union of word and flesh, set him free.

He was twenty-two as he took to the open road and then sailed for transoceanic ports. In South America he remained less than a year. This voyage and return were to have a vital impact on his writing. He entered the world of hobos, clowns, beggars, itinerants. In the Argentine he worked as a gaucho, miner, stoker, fireman with police duties. He became a tumbler in a circus and its janitor. In the maritime provinces, he tempered steel, played the triangle in an orchestra, groomed horses, cranked a barrel-organ. He was also a pianist in a nightclub. Had arithmetic not failed him, he said not without humor to his physician at Castel Pulci, he might have become a clerk or a bookkeeper. As no job could hold him, he could hold no job. Driven by hobomania, he was thrust from place to place to worlds he could not fit into.

After these misadventures in adversity, he hankered for home. Unable to induce his father to send him passage, he stowed away on a freighter. At sea he learned his destination was Odessa. There he joined the Bossiaki, a Gypsy tribe that worked the fairs in groups of five to six outcasts. He shipped out to Genoa where "The Tyrrhenian night was a devastation of innumerable eyes!" With a poet's second sight he caught the vibrancy of the great port and made a seaman's voyage to Antwerp. He returned home by way of Rotterdam, Paris, and Basel, not without imprisonment for vagrancy and internment in an asylum when a magistrate with human understanding recognized in him signs of madness.

In Marradi Campana tramped the mountain trails. For days he walked along the face of La Verna. It took him a week to cross La Falterona to reach a sanctuary hidden in its recesses. In these mountain hideouts, he confronted the tortured creatures of his imagination when the world was too much for him to bear. It may have been that his father's brusqueness now softened and the persuasive advice of the pharmacist Ciottoli directed him to the university again, this time not for chemistry pure but for pharmaceutical studies. These desires were dissipated and completely unrealized. Dino transferred from one university to another, gave up Bologna for Genoa, Genoa for the Institute in Florence, and within a year of his degree, Florence for an art no one could teach anyone, poetry.

Campana had kept a *Notebook* (*Quaderno*). He put these poems aside and in a burst of writing that autumn, in 1914, produced *Orphic Songs*, completing the work in a few weeks.

By December he had a book as unique as himself. His primitive nature with overpowering fantasy had created a poetry at once disordered, anarchic, perverse. With his manuscript secure, he trudged the forty miles from Marradi across the mountain gap to Florence.

Florence had publishing houses. Reputations were made at the cafés. In the Piazza Vittorio, now the Piazza della Repubblica, there was always good talk as exciting controversies on art, literature, politics raged. Café Paszkowski and Giubbe Rosse across the square catered to the literati, the artists, and the journalists. Spirited young men who dominated this intellectual milieu had founded *La Voce*, a superlative weekly newspaper. They were in their twenties. So was Campana. When he met Soffici, the Futurist painter, and Papini, man of letters, he told them he had hiked from Marradi to give them his poems and to ask for their judgment. Soffici observed how thickset and sturdy Dino was in his seaman's greatcoat. He noted the wide-jawed face, the hair and beard fiery-red, the blue eyes, sincere, if fearful and ardent. In his journal Soffici recalled, "He drew from his pocket an old notebook covered with rough and dirty paper, the kind used by dealers and farmers in toting up accounts . . . ."

In Marradi, Campana waited for word that never came. No news of even one acceptance for *La Voce*, let alone the recommendation of his poetry to the respectable publishing houses. When Papini stepped down from his editorship in favor of Prezzolini, the journalist and scholar who had first held the office, Dino pleaded for a hearing. There was no

answer to his letter. In desperation he appealed to Soffici for the return of *Orphic Songs*, saying he had no other copy and that he intended to publish the poetry himself. In one of those tragedies that overcome genius, Campana heard directly from Soffici that he had lost the manuscript in moving to new quarters. The hurt was deep; what saved him from utter derangement was his unyielding will to survive as poet. In a fury he rewrote *Orphic Songs* from memory that spring of 1914 and saw it through the press in the local printshop above Ciottoli's pharmacy in Marradi.

That summer *Orphic Songs* was displayed in a Florentine bookstore. Soffici saw it in the window and with a feeling of remorse at his carelessness and negligence, went in and bought a copy. He was overwhelmed by its dark power, morbid insights, and raw beauty. He sent a letter of great praise to Campana, who had also received encomium in a review by Emilio Cecchi, poet and critic. This was enough reason for Dino to return to Florence. The welcome he received was not sanguine; the compliments were polite, if not too warm. He stood at the periphery of a literary circle that did not take him in.

Among the crowded tables at the cafés he offered copies for sale. Patrons who bought these books out of charity may have sensed each merciful act was salt on an open wound. Unaware he was the butt of jokesters, who demanded documentary proof he was a poet, he withdrew from his breastpocket his precious papers: Soffici's letter and Cecchi's review. In his naïveté he read them aloud to the smug, all-

knowing listeners. A wag among the journalists started a rumor that gave credence to Campana's madness: he never autographed a copy for a café patron whose face did not favorably impress him, but in anger ripped out poems he was sure the buyer lacked the intelligence to understand. Years later at Castel Pulci, he gave the lie to the journalists whose exaggerations he understandingly excused, saying simply he sold his books because he was hungry.

In breaking the fetters of an enslaving culture, the poet Dino Campana delighted only a handful of the avant-garde of his generation. Right at its heels there was another, the young, who took to heart this poetry written at white heat from memory. For all its agrammatical and ungrammatical structure, its hiatuses and unfilled brackets (as if a thought were blown away never to be recaptured), this was a poetry for Italy's youth. They could feel it in their bones. Their Campana had created his own aesthetic and developed a sense of tone-color never before experienced in Italian poetry. Throughout his work there were key words integral to his sense of sound, words singularly his own: *taciturn, nocturnal, ambiguous, dizziness, serene.* Here was a poetry unshackled and unchecked, nothing in it dependent on tricks and techniques. In his poetry there was an otherworldly music and unearthly splendor so like the dark landscape of Thule, Poe's ultimate dim dreamland. If Poe's imaginative vision infused *Orphic Songs*, Whitman left an even stronger mark in a few phrases directly translated: *Faint creaking of cordage* became *un dolce scricchiolìo*, just as *hankering, gross, mystical,* and

nude found an altered variant in *Nude mystical up high hollow*, and *O book! fulfil your destiny!* had its counterpart in *O sea prepare my destiny*.

. . .

There is a sense of loneliness and abandonment in his poetry, as if in a brutish world, halved by the light of madness and the dark of sanity, he groped for the cold asylum of eternity. Called up by the army, he was declared mentally unbalanced. Within weeks of these findings he was classified as hopelessly insane and admitted to Castel Pulci.

In the fourteen years that Campana ate at the common table, he was alone. In the anteroom to the ward where he was one of several, his bed against the wall relieved by a barred window well out of reach, he was alone. In an isolated cubicle, he carried on correspondence with Soffici, Cecchi, and Binazzi, the editor of the second edition of *Orphic Songs*. He felt himself apart from everything about him, ever a loner, at one with the universe, if not with men, in closing "Metaphors for a Journey and a Mountain":

> Here is the night and here to watch me
> Lights and lights: and I far off and alone:
> The harvest is quiet, against infinity
> (Quiet is the spirit) mute lyrics go
> Into the night: to the night: I listen. I
> Who had departed am nothing but a shadow come
>   back . . .

He lies in the little church of Badia a Settimo. He had been buried in the cemetery of San Colombo, nearby. His remains were moved to the plot in front of the campanile. When this was bombed by the Nazis, he was interred under a slab of bluish sandstone with these words incised:

DINO CAMPANA

Poet

1885–1932

The marks of his insanity are like stigmata on the corpus of his work.

I. L. Salomon
New York, N.Y.

from

ORPHIC SONGS

LA CHIMERA

Non so se tra roccie il tuo pallido
Viso m'apparve, o sorriso
Di lontananze ignote
Fosti, la china eburnea
Fronte fulgente o giovine
Suora de la Gioconda:
O delle primavere
Spente, per i tuoi mitici pallori
O Regina o Regina adolescente:
Ma per il tuo ignoto poema
Di voluttà e di dolore
Musica fanciulla esangue,
Segnato di linea di sangue
Nel cerchio delle labbra sinuose,
Regina de la melodia:
Ma per il vergine capo
Reclino, io poeta notturno
Vegliai le stelle vivide nei pelaghi del cielo.
Io per il tuo dolce mistero
Io per il tuo divenir taciturno.
Non so se la fiamma pallida
Fu dei capelli il vivente
Segno del suo pallore,
Non so se fu un dolce vapore,
Dolce sul mio dolore,

THE CHIMERA

I do not know if among the rocks
Your pallid face appeared to me
Or if you were the smile
Of unknown distances,
Your slanted ivory brow radiant
O young sister to La Gioconda:
O for your mythical pallor
Of dead springs, O Queen
O adolescent Queen:
But for your unknown poem
Of voluptuousness and grief
Ashen-faced musical girl
Marked with a line of blood
Encircled in sinuous lips,
Queen of song:
But for your virgin head inclined,
I poet of the night
Kept watch of the bright stars in the seas of the sky.
I for your sweet mystery
I for your taciturn becoming.
I do not know if the pale flame
Of your hair was the living
Sign of your pallor.
I do not know if it was a sweet haze,
Sweet to my grief,

3

Sorriso di un volto notturno:
Guardo le bianche rocce le mute fonti dei venti
E l'immobilità dei firmamenti
E i gonfii rivi che vanno piangenti
E l'ombre del lavoro umano curve là sui poggi
        algenti
E ancora per teneri cieli lontane chiare ombre correnti
E ancora ti chiamo ti chiamo Chimera.

Smile of a face in the night:
I look at the white rocks the mute sources of the winds
And the immobility of firmaments
And the swollen streams that go weeping
And the shadows of laborers curved there on the ice-cold
      hills
And too distant bright shadows running through soft skies
And still I call you call you Chimera.

GIARDINO AUTUNNALE

(Firenze)

Al giardino spettrale al lauro muto
De le verdi ghirlande
A la terra autunnale
Un ultimo saluto!
A l'aride pendici
Aspre arrossate nell'estremo sole
Confusa di rumori
Rauchi grida la lontana vita:
Grida al morente sole
Che insanguina le aiole.
S'intende una fanfara
Che straziante sale: il fiume spare
Ne le arene dorate: nel silenzio
Stanno le bianche statue a capo i ponti
Volte: e le cosa già non sono più.
E dal fondo silenzio come un coro
Tenero e grandioso
Sorge ed anela in alto al mio balcone:
E in aroma d'alloro,
In aroma d'alloro acre languente,
Tra le statue immortali nel tramonto
Ella m'appar, presente.

AUTUMNAL GARDEN

(Florence)

To the spectral garden to the silenced laurel
With green garlands
To autumnal earth
A last goodby!
On the harsh barren
Reddened hillsides in the waning sun
Life in the distance
Its raucous cries merged screams:
Screams to the dying sun
That stains the flowerbeds with blood.
A piercing fanfare is heard
Rising: the river disappears
Into the golden sand: the white statues
Turned toward the head of the bridges stand
In the silence: and already things no longer are.
And from the depth silence like a tender
And impressive chorus rises
And gasps high up to my balcony:
And in the laurel scent,
In the sharp lingering laurel scent
Among the immortal statues in the sunset
She appears to me, now.

L'INVETRIATA

La sera fumosa d'estate
Dall'alta invetriata mesce chiarori nell'ombra
E mi lascia nel cuore un suggello ardente.
Ma chi ha (sul terrazzo sul fiume si accende una lampada)
      chi ha
A la Madonnina del Ponte chi è chi è che ha acceso la
      lampada?—c'è
Nella stanza un odor di putredine: c'è
Nella stanza una piaga rossa languente.
Le stelle sono bottoni di madreperla e la sera si veste di
      velluto:
E tremola la sera fatua: è fatua la sera e
      tremola ma c'è
Nel cuore della sera c'è,
Sempre una piaga rossa languente.

THE GLASS WINDOW

From the upper glass window the smoky summer evening
Pours brightness upon shadow
That leaves on my heart a burning seal.
But who has (on the terrace on the river a lamp is lit)
      who has
Who is he who has lit the lamp at the Little Madonna of
      the Bridge?—there is
In the room a smell of putrefaction: there is
In the room a red stagnant wound.
The stars are buttons of mother-of-pearl and the evening is
      clothed in velvet:
The fatuous evening trembles: fatuous is the evening and it
      trembles but there is
At the heart of evening there is
Ever a red stagnant wound.

IL CANTO DELLA TENEBRA

La luce del crepuscolo si attenua:
Inquieti spiriti sia dolce la tenebra
Al cuore che non ama più!
Sorgenti sorgenti abbiam da ascoltare,
Sorgenti, sorgenti che sanno
Sorgenti che sanno che spiriti stanno
Che spiriti stanno a ascoltare . . .
Ascolta: la luce del crepuscolo attenua
Ed agli inquieti spiriti è dolce la tenebra:
Ascolta: ti ha vinto la Sorte:
Ma per i cuori leggeri un'altra vita è alle porte:
Non c'è di dolcezza che possa uguagliare la Morte
Più Più Più
Intendi chi ancora ti culla:
Intendi la dolce fanciulla
Che dice all'orecchio: Più Più
Ed ecco si leva e scompare
Il vento: ecco torna dal mare
Ed ecco sentiamo ansimare
Il cuore che ci amò di più!
Guardiamo: di già il paesaggio
Degli alberi e l'acque è notturno
Il fiume va via taciturno. . . .
Pùm! mamma quell'omo lassù!

SONG OF DARKNESS

The light of dusk draws thin:
Disquieted spirits may darkness be sweet
To the heart that no longer loves!
Springs at the source we have to listen to,
Springs, springs that know
Springs that know that spirits are
That spirits are listening. . . .
Listen: the light of dusk thins
And to the disquieted spirits darkness is sweet:
Listen: Fate has vanquished you:
But for the light of heart another life is at the door:
No More More More
Is there gentleness that can equalize Death
Understand who still cradles you:
Understand the sweet girl
Who whispers into your ear: No More More
And here the wind rises and disappears:
Here it returns from the sea
And here we listen to the gasping heart
That loved us more!
Let us look: already the landscape
Of trees and water is nocturnal
The river goes its taciturn way. . . .
Bang! Mama, that man up there!

LA VERNA (DIARIO)

II. RITORNO

Salgo (nello spazio, fuori del tempo)

L'acqua il vento
La sanità delle prime cose —
Il lavoro umano sull'elemento
Liquido — la natura che conduce
Strati di rocce su strati — il vento
Che scherza nella valle — ed ombra del vento
La nuvola — il lontano ammonimento
Del fiume nella valle —
E la rovina del contrafforte — la frana
La vittoria dell'elemento — il vento
Che scherza nella valle.
Su la lunghissima valle che sale in scale
La casetta di sasso sul faticoso verde:
La bianca immagine dell'elemento.

La tellurica melodia della Falterona. Le onde telluriche.
L'ultimo asterisco della melodia della Falterona s'inselva nella
nuvole. Su la costa lontana traluce la linea vittoriosa dei gio-
vani abeti, l'avanguardia dei giganti giovinetti serrati in
battaglia, felici nel sole lungo la lunga costa torrenziale. In
fondo, nel frusciar delle nere selve sempre più avanti accam-

MOUNT VERNA (DIARY)

II. RETURN

I leap (into space outside of time)

Water wind
Soundness of first things—
Human work on the liquid
Element—nature that directs
Strata of rocks on strata—the wind
That plays in the valley—and shadow of the wind
the cloud—the distant warning
of the river in the valley—
And the ruin of the buttress—the landslide
Victor over the element—the wind
That plays in the valley.
Up the longest valley that rises gradually
The little stone house under weary greenness:
The white image of the element.

The telluric song of the Falterona. The telluric waves.
The final admonition of the Falterona's song hides itself in
clouds as in the woods. On the distant slope the triumphant
line of the young firs glistens, the vanguard of the gigantic
young, serried in battle, radiant in the sun along the long
torrential slope. At the base in the rustling of the black

panti lo scoglio enorme che si ripiega grottesco su sé stesso, pachiderma a quattro zampe sotto la massa oscura: la Verna. E varco e varco.

Campigno: paese barbarico, fuggente, paese notturno, mistico incubo del caos. Il tuo abitante porge la notte dell' antico animale umano nei suoi gesti. Nelle tue mosse montagne l'elemento grottesco profila: un gaglioffo, una grossa puttana fuggono sotto le nubi in corsa. E le tue rive bianche come le nubi, triangolari, curve come gonfie vele: paese barbarico, fuggente, paese notturno, mistico incubo del Caos.

.   .   .   .

Monte Filetto, 25 Settembre

Un usignolo canta tra i rami del noce. Il poggio è troppo bello sul cielo troppo azzurro. Il fiume canta bene la sua cantilena. È un'ora che guardo lo spazio laggiù e la strada a mezza costa del poggio che vi conduce. Quassù abitano i falchi. La pioggia leggera d'estate batteva come un ricco accordo sulle foglie del noce. Ma le foglie dell'acacia albero caro alla notte si piegavano senza rumore come un'ombra verde. L'azzurro si apre tra questi due alberi. Il noce è davanti alla finestra della mia stanza. Di notte sembra raccogliere tutta l'ombra e curvare le cupe foglie canore come una messe di canti sul tronco rotondo lattiginoso quasi umano: l'acacia sa profilarsi come un chimerico fumo. Le stelle danzavano sul poggio deserto. Nessuno viene per la strada. Mi piace dai balconi guardare la campagna deserta

woods ever more encamped in front the enormous grotesque rock communes with itself, a pachyderm on four talons under the obscure mass. Verna. I will cross and surmount.

Campigno: barbaric country, transient, nocturnal country, mystic incubus of chaos. Your inhabitant presents the night of the ancient animal, human in his gestures. In your mountain movements the grotesque element is outlined: a blockhead and a fat whore fly under the running clouds. And your white banks like the clouds, triangular, curved like swollen sails: barbaric country, transient, nocturnal country, mystic incubus of Chaos.

.   .   .   .

Mount Filetto, September 25

A nightingale sings in the branches of the walnut tree. The hilltop is too beautiful against a sky too blue. The river sings its singsong well. It is a moment when I look at the space down below and the street halfway up the slope that takes me there. Up here the hawks live. The light summer rain pattered a rich tune on the walnut leaves. But the leaves of the acacia dear to the night yielded without sound as a green shadow. There is open sky between these two trees. The walnut is in front of the window of my room. At night it seems to gather the entire shadow and to curve its dark melodious leaves like a harvest of songs around its milky almost human trunk: the acacia knows how to appear in profile as illusory smoke. The stars danced on the deserted hilltop. No one comes down the street. From the balcony I like to look at the lonely field with

15

abitata da alberi sparsi, anima della solitudine forgiata di vento. Oggi che il cielo e il paesaggio erano così dolci dopo la pioggia pensavo alle signorine di Maupassant e di Jammes chine l'ovale pallido sulla tappezzeria memore e sulle stampe. Il fiume riprende la sua cantilena. Vado via. Guardo ancora la finestra: la costa è un quadretto d'oro nello squittire dei falchi.

Presso Campigno, 26 Settembre

.   .   .   .

Ecco le rocce, strati su strati, monumenti di tenacia solitaria che consolano il cuore degli uomini. E dolce mi è sembrato il mio destino fuggitivo al fascino dei lontani miraggi di ventura che ancora arridono dai monti azzurri: e a udire il sussurrare dell'acqua sotto le nude roccie, fresca ancora delle profondità della terra. Così conosco una musica dolce nel mio ricordo senza ricordarmene neppure una nota: so che si chiama la partenza o il ritorno: conosco un quadro perduto tra lo splendore dell'arte fiorentina colla sua parola di dolce nostalgia: è il figliuol prodigo all'ombra degli alberi della casa paterna. Letteratura? Non so. Il mio ricordo, l'acqua è così. Dopo gli sfondi spirituali senza spirito, dopo l'oro crepuscolare, dolce come il canto dell'onnipresente tenebra è il canto dell'acqua sotto le rocce: così come è dolce l'elemento nello splendore nero degli occhi delle vergini spagnole: e come le corde delle chitarre di Spagna . . . Ribera, dove vidi le tue danze arieggiate di secchi accordi? Il tuo satiro aguzzo alla danza dei vittoriosi accordi? E in contro l'altra tua faccia,

16

its scattered trees, the soul of solitude forged by the wind. Today when the sky and country were so sweet after the rain, I thought of the young ladies in de Maupassant and in Jammes, their pallid oval faces bowed in pleasing tapestry and in engravings. The river takes up its singsong again. I will go away. Again I look through the window: the slope is a little golden square under the squeaking hawks.

Near Campigno, September 26

.   .   .   .

Look at the rocks, strata on strata, monuments of solitary toughness that comfort the heart of man. And my fugitive destiny seemed sweet to me under the spell of distant illusions that fortunately still shine down from the blue mountains: to hear under the bare rocks the whisper of water still fresh from the depths of the earth. So in my memory I am aware of sweet music without my remembering even one note: I know it is called departure or return: I know of a painting lost in the brilliance of Florentine art with its word of sweet nostalgia: it is the prodigal son in the shadow of trees of his paternal house. Literature? I do not know. My remembrance: this is what water is. After the spiritual backgrounds without soul, after the golden twilight, sweet as the song of darkness everywhere is the song of water under the rocks: so is there a sweet element in the black brilliant eyes of Spanish virgins: and like the strings of Spanish guitars . . . Ribera, where did I see your airy dances to harsh chords? Your pointed satyr dancing to triumphant chords? And opposed to your face the horseman of

il cavaliere della morte, l'altra tua faccia cuore profondo, cuore danzante, satiro cinto di pampini danzante sulla sacra oscenità di Sileno? Nude scheletriche stampe, sulla rozza parete in un meriggio torrido fantasmi della pietra. . . .

.   .   .   .

Ascolto. Le fontane hanno taciuto nella voce del vento. Dalla roccia cola un filo d'acqua in un incavo. Il vento allenta e raffrena il morso del lontano dolore. Ecco son volto. Tra le rocce crepuscolari una forma nera cornuta immobile mi guarda immobile con occhi d'oro.

.   .   .   .

Laggiù nel crepuscolo la pianura di Romagna. O donna sognata, donna adorata, donna forte, profilo nobilitato di un ricordo di immobilità bizantina, in linee dolci e potenti testa nobile e mitica dorata dell'enigma delle sfingi: occhi crepuscolari in paesaggio di torri là sognati sulle rive della guerreggiata pianura, sulle rive dei fiumi bevuti dalla terra avida là dove si perde il grido di Francesca: dalla mia fanci-ullezza una voce liturgica risuonava in preghiera lenta e commossa: e tu da quel ritmo sacro a me commosso sorgevi, già inquieto di vaste pianure, di lontani miracolosi destini: risveglia la mia speranza sull'infinito della pianura o del mare sentendo aleggiare un soffio di grazia: nobiltà carnale e dorata, profondità dorata degli occhi: guerriera, amante, mistica, benigna di nobiltà umana antica Romagna.

.   .   .   .

death, your other face heart deep, heart dancing, satyr girded with vine leaves dancing on the holy obscenity of Silenus? Naked skeletal shapes on the rough cliff one scorching afternoon, phantasms of stone. . . .

. . . .

I listen. Against the wind's speech the fountains have fallen silent. From the rock a trickle of water drips into the hollow. The wind slackens and curbs the sting of distant grief. Here I am turned about. Among the dusky rocks a black horned motionless figure with golden eyes looks at motionless me.

. . . .

Down there in the twilight the flatland of Romagna. O woman desired, woman adored, vigorous woman, profile distinguished by a remembrance of Byzantine immobility, in smooth and strong lines noble and golden mythic head like the enigma of a sphinx: eyes crepuscular in sight of towers imagined there on the banks of the battleground on the banks of rivers gulped down by the eager earth there where Francesca's scream is lost: from my childhood a liturgical voice resounded in slow and touching prayer: and from that holy rhythm touched by me you arose, already restless for the vast plains, for distant miraculous destiny: my hope awakens on the infinity of the plain or of the sea feeling a puff of grace flutter: carnal and golden nobility, golden profundity of eyes: warrior, lover, mystic, benign in nobility O human ancient Romagna.

. . . .

L'acqua del mulino corre piana e invisibile nella gora. Rivedo un fanciullo, lo stesso fanciullo, laggiù steso sull' erba. Sembra dormire. Ripenso alla mia fanciullezza: quanto tempo è trascorso da quando i bagliori magnetici delle stelle mi dissero per la prima volta dell'infinità delle morti! . . . Il tempo è scorso, si è addensato, è scorso: così come l'acque scorre, immobile per quel fanciullo: lasciando dietro a sé il silenzio, la gora profonda e uguale: conservando il silenzio come ogni giorno l'ombra. . . .

Quel fanciullo o quella immagine proiettata dalla mia nostalgia? Così immobile laggiù: come il mio cadavere.

Marradi (Antica volta. Specchio velato)

Il mattino arride sulle cime dei monti. In alto sulle cuspidi di un triangolo desolato si illumina il castello, più alto e più lontano. Venere passa in barroccio accoccolata per la strada conventuale. Il fiume si snoda per la valle: rotto e muggente a tratti canta e riposa in larghi specchi d'azzurro: e più veloce trascorre le mura nere (una cupola rossa ride lontana con il suo leone) e i campanili si affollano e nel nereggiare inquieto dei tetti al sole una lunga veranda che ha messo un commento variopinto di archi!

Presso Marradi (ottobre)

Son capitato in mezzo a bona gente. La finestra della mia stanza che affronta i venti: e la . . . e il figlio, povero uccellino dai tratti dolci e dall'anima indecisa, povero uccellino che trascina una gamba rotta, e il vento che batte alla finestra dall'orizzonte annuvolato, i monti lontani ed alti,

Slow and invisible the water flows into the millstream. Again I see a boy, the same boy, down there stretched out on the grass. He seems asleep. I recall my childhood: how much time has passed since the magnetic rays of the stars spoke to me for the first time from the infinity of the dead! . . . . The time is past, is thickened, is gone: so it flows like the water motionless for that boy: leaving behind him silence, the deep and level millpond: conserving silence just as everyday shadow. . . .

That boy or that likeness projected by my nostalgia? So motionless down there: like my corpse.

Marradi (Ancient time. Veiled mirror)

On the mountain peaks the morning is bright. Up high on the pinnacles of a desolate triangle the castle higher and farther off appears. A girl, Venus, crouched in a cart goes down the street of the convent. The river unwinds through the valley: broken and roaring at times it sings and rests in widening blue mirrors: and more swiftly it runs along the black walls (a red cupola with its lion glistens far off) and the bell towers are crowded and in the blackening unquiet of the roofs in the sun a long veranda has written a many-colored comment on the arches!

Close by Marradi (October)

I have come upon decent people. The window of my room faces the winds: and the . . . the son, poor little bird sweet-mannered and indecisive of spirit, poor little bird who drags a broken leg, and the wind from the clouded horizon

21

il rombo monotono del vento. Lontano è caduta la neve. . . .
La padrona zitta mi rifà il letto aiutata dalla fanticella.
Monotona dolcezza della vita patriarcale. Fine del pellegri-
naggio.

beats at the window, from the distant and high mountains the monotonous rumble of the wind. Far-off the snow has fallen. . . . Silently the owner helped by her little servant makes up my bed. Dull gentleness of the patriarchal life. End of the pilgrimage.

IMMAGINI DEL VIAGGIO
E DELLA MONTAGNA

. . . . poi che nella sorda lotta notturna
La più potente anima seconda ebbe frante le nostre catene
Noi ci svegliammo piangendo ed era l'azzurro mattino:
Come ombre d'eroi veleggiavano:
De l'alba non ombre nei puri silenzii
De l'alba
Nei puri pensieri
Non ombre
De l'alba non ombre:
Piangendo: giurando noi fede all'azzurro

.   .   .   .

.   .   .   .

Pare la donna che siede pallida giovine ancora
Sopra dell'erta ultima presso la casa antica:
Avanti a lei incerte si snodano le valli
Verso le solitudini alte de gli orizzonti:
La gentile canuta il cuculo sente a cantare.
E il semplice cuore provato negli anni
A le melodie della terra
Ascolta quieto: le note
Giungon, continue ambigue come in un velo di seta.
Da selve oscure il torrente
Sorte ed in torpidi gorghi la chiostra di rocce
Lambe ed involge aereo cilestrino. . . .

METAPHORS FOR A JOURNEY
AND A MOUNTAIN

. . . . after the nocturnal hidden struggle
The more powerful second soul had broken our chains
We awoke crying and it was a sky-blue morning:
Like shadows of heroes they sailed:
Of the dawn no shadows in the pure silences
Of the dawn
In pure thoughts
No shadows
Of the dawn no shadows:
Weeping: we swore our faith to the sky

.   .   .   .

.   .   .   .

The pale woman who sits on the last slope
Near the ancient house still looks like a young girl:
Before her the valleys unwind uncertainly
Toward the steep solitudes on the horizons:
The kind old woman hears the cuckoo singing.
And the simple heart tested through the years
By the songs of the earth
Listens quietly: the notes
Reach her, continually ambiguously as in a silken veil.
From dim woods the torrent
Moves off and in sluggish eddies skims the boundary
Of rocks and envelops the airy blue. . . .

E il cuculo cola più lento due note velate
Nel silenzio azzurrino

.   .   .   .

.   .   .   .

L'aria ride: la tromba a valle i monti
Squilla: la massa degli scorridori
Si scioglie: ha vivi lanci: i nostri cuori
Balzano: e grida ed oltrevarca i ponti.
E dalle altezze agli infiniti albori
Vigili, calan trepidi pei monti,
Tremuli e vaghi nelle vive fonti,
Gli echi dei nostri due sommessi cuori. . . .
Hanno varcato in lunga teoria:
Nell'aria non so qual bacchico canto
Salgono: e dietro a loro il monte introna:

.   .   .   .

E si distingue il loro verde canto.

.   .   .   .

Andar, *de l'acque ai gorghi*, per la china
Valle, *nel sordo mormorar sfiorato:*
Seguire un'ala stanca per la china
Valle che batte e volge: desolato
Andar per valli, in fin che in azzurrina
Serenità, dall'aspre rocce dato
Un Borgo in grigio e vario torreggiare
All'alterno pensier pare e dispare,
Sovra l'arido sogno, serenato!
O se come il torrente che rovina

And the cuckoo trickles two veiled notes
Quite slowly into the pale blue silence

.   .   .   .

.   .   .   .

The air laughs: in the valley a trumpet blares
To the mountains: the group of raiders
Dissolves: they fly in lively leaps: our hearts
Jump: they shriek and cross beyond the bridges.
And from heights to infinite dawns
The echoes of our two humble hearts
Watchful apprehensive swoop down the mountains,
Tremulous and vague in lively fountains. . . .
They have passed through a sweeping line:
I do not know what Bacchic song they rise to
In the air: behind them the mountain thunders:

.   .   .   .

And their green song is distinguishable.

.   .   .   .

To go, *from waters to whirlpools*, through the valley's
Slope, *into the hovering muffled murmur*:
To follow down the sloping valley a tired wing
That beats and turns: to go desolate
Through valleys until in pale blue serenity
A gray little village with varying towers
Emerging from sharp rocks
Appears and disappears to our alternate thoughts
Above our arid dream, cloudless!
O if as the torrent that collapses

27

E si riposa nell'azzurro eguale,
Se tale a le tue mura la proclina
Anima al nulla nel suo andar fatale,
Se alle tue mura in pace cristallina
Tender potessi, in una pace uguale,
E il ricordo specchiar di una divina
Serenità perduta o tu immortale
Anima! o Tu!

.   .   .   .

.   .   .   .

La messe, intesa al misterioso coro
Del vento, in vie di lunghe onde tranquille
Muta e gloriosa per le mie pupille
Discioglie il grembo delle luci d'oro.
O Speranza! O Speranza! a mille a mille
Splendono nell'estate i frutti! un coro
Ch'è incantato, è al suo murmure, canoro
Che vive per miriadi di faville! . . .

Ecco la notte: ed ecco vigilarmi
E luci e luci: ed io lontano e solo:
Quieta è la messe, verso l'infinito
(Quieto è lo spirto) vanno muti carmi
A la notte: a la notte: intendo: Solo
Ombra che torna, ch'era dipartito. . . .

And stays under a changeless sky,
As at your walls the spirit inclines
To nothing in its fatal going,
If at your walls in crystalline peace
I could stretch out in an identical peace
And reflect the remembrance of a divine
Serenity lost O you immortal
Soul! O you!

.   .   .   .

.   .   .   .

Attentive to the mysterious choir of the wind
Down paths of long tranquil waves
The harvest, mute and glorious, before my eyes
Undoes the bosom of her golden lights.
O Hope! O Hope! By the thousands
Fruits glisten in summer! A choir
That is enchanted is in its murmur melodious
And lives by myriad sparks! . . .

Here is the night and here to watch me
Lights and lights: and I far off and alone:
The harvest is quiet, against infinity
(Quiet is the spirit) mute lyrics go
Into the night: to the night: I listen: I
Who had departed am nothing but a shadow come back. . . .

VIAGGIO A MONTEVIDEO

Io vidi dal ponte della nave
I colli di Spagna
Svanire, nel verde
Dentro il crepuscolo d'oro la bruna terra celando
Come una melodia:
D'ignota scena fanciulla sola
Come una melodia
Blu, su la riva dei colli ancora tremare una viola. . . .
Illanguidiva la sera celeste sul mare:
Pure i dorati silenzii ad ora ad ora dell'ale
Varcaron lentamente in un azzurreggiare: . . .
Lontani tinti dei varii colori
Dai più lontani silenzii
Ne la celeste sera varcaron gli uccelli d'oro: la nave
Già cieca varcando battendo la tenebra
Coi nostri naufraghi cuori
Battendo la tenebra l'ale celeste sul mare.
Ma un giorno
Salirono sopra la nave le gravi matrone di Spagna
Da gli occhi torbidi e angelici
Dai seni gravidi di vertigine. Quando
In una baia profonda di un'isola equatoriale
In una baia tranquilla e profonda assai più del cielo notturno
Noi vedemmo sorgere nella luce incantata
Una bianca città addormentata

JOURNEY TO MONTEVIDEO

From the deck of the ship I saw
The hills of Spain
Disappear, the golden twilight
Hiding the brown earth in the green
Like a song:
Like a blue song
Of a lonely girl from an unknown place,
A violet still trembling on the bank of the hills. . . .
The azure evening languished on the sea:
Even the golden silences of wings
Crossed slowly minute by minute in blueness. . . .
Distant golden birds tinged
In varicolored hues crossed the heavenly evening
From more distant silences: the ship
Already blind crossing battering the darkness
With our shipwrecked hearts
Battering the darkness, its azure wings on the sea.
But one day
The solemn matrons from Spain climbed aboard the ship
With turbid and angelic eyes
And breasts heavy with vertigo. When
In a deep bay of an equatorial island
In a quiet bay much more profound than the nocturnal sky
We saw rising in the bewitching light
A white city asleep

Ai piedi dei picchi altissimi dei vulcani spenti
Nel soffio torbido dell'equatore: finché
Dopo molte grida e molte ombre di un paese
  ignoto,
Dopo molto cigolìo di catene e molto acceso fervore
Noi lasciammo la città equatoriale
Verso l'inquieto mare notturno.
Andavamo andavamo, per giorni e per giorni: le navi
Gravi di vele molli di caldi soffi incontro passavano lente:
Sì presso di sul cassero a noi ne appariva bronzina
Una fanciulla della razza nuova,
Occhi lucenti e le vesti al vento! ed ecco: selvaggia a la fine di un
  giorno che apparve
La riva selvaggia là giù sopra la sconfinata
  marina:
E vidi come cavalle
Vertiginose che si scioglievano le dune
Verso la prateria senza fine
Deserta senza le case umane
E noi volgemmo fuggendo le dune che apparve
Su un mare giallo de la portentosa dovizia del
  fiume,
Del continente nuovo la capitale marina.
Limpido fresco ed elettrico era il lume
Della sera e là le alte case parevan deserte
Laggiù sul mar del pirata
De la città abbandonata
Tra il mare giallo e le dune . . . . . .

At the foot of the highest peaks of the dead volcanoes
In the equator's turbid breath: till
After much screaming and many shadows in an unknown
      country
After much clattering of chains and much inflamed fervor
We left the equatorial city
For the restless nocturnal sea.
We went on and on for days and days: the ships
Heavy with sails limp in the hot gusts of wind passed opposite us slowly:
Nearby on the upper deck there appeared a bronzed
Girl of a new race,
Eyes shining, her clothes to the wind! and here:
      wild at day's end
There appeared the wild shore down there next to the
      endless sea:
And I saw the dunes
Like dizzy horses that dissolved
Into limitless grassland
Deserted without houses for anyone
And we turned flying from the dunes and there appeared
On a yellow floodtide of the miraculous abundance of the
      river
The marine capital of the new continent.
Limpid fresh and electric was the light
Of evening and there the tall houses seemed deserted
Down below on the pirate's sea
Of the abandoned city
Between the yellow sea and the dunes   .   .   .   .

FANTASIA
SU UN QUADRO D'ARDENGO SOFFICI

Faccia, zig zag anatomico che oscura
La passione torva di una vecchia luna
Che guarda sospesa al soffitto
In una taverna café chantant
D'America: la rossa velocità
Di luci *funambola che tanga*
Spagnola cinerina
Isterica in tango di luci si disfà:
Che guarda nel café chantant
D'America:
Sul piano martellato tre
Fiammelle rosse si sono accese da sé.

FANTASY ON A PAINTING
BY ARDENGO SOFFICI

Face, anatomic zigzag that eclipses
The grim passion of an old moon
That watches suspended from the ceiling
In a tavern like an American
Cabaret: the red kinetic
Of lights *a rope-walker who tangoes*
A Spanish olive-ashen girl
Hysterically dissolves in a tango of lights:
That watches in the American
Cabaret:
On the pounded floor three
Red flames light up by themselves.

DUALISMO
(Lettera Aperta a Manuelita Etchegarray)

Voi adorabile creola dagli occhi neri e scintillanti come metallo in fusione, voi figlia generosa della prateria nutrita di aria vergine voi tornate ad apparirmi col ricordo lontano: anima dell'oasi dove la mia vita ritrovò un istante il contatto delle forze del cosmo. Io vi rivedo Manuelita, il piccolo viso armato dell'ala battagliera del vostro cappello, la piuma di struzzo avvolta e ondulante eroicamente, i vostri piccoli passi pieni di slancio contenuto sopra il terreno delle promesse eroiche! Tutta mi siete presente esile e nervosa. La cipria sparsa come neve sul vostro viso consunto da un fuoco interno, le vostre vesti di rosa che proclamano la vostra verginità come un'aurora piena di promesse! E ancora il magnetismo di quando voi chinaste il capo, voi fiore meraviglioso di una razza eroica, mi attira non ostante il tempo ancora verso di voi! Eppure Manuelita sappiatelo se lo potete: *io non pensavo, non pensavo a voi: io mai non ho pensato a voi.* Di notte nella piazza deserta, quando nuvole vaghe correvano verso strane costellazioni, alla triste luce elettrica io sentivo la mia infinita solitudine. La prateria si alzava come un mare argentato agli sfondi, e rigetti di quel mare, miseri, uomini feroci, uomini ignoti chiusi nel loro cupo volere, storie sanguinose subito dimenticate che rivivevano improvvisamente nella notte, tessevano attorno a me la storia della città giovine e feroce, conquistatrice implacabile, ardente di

DUALISM
(Open letter to Manuelita Etchegarray)

You adorable Creole with eyes black and scintillating like metal in fusion, you generous daughter of the grassland nurtured by untainted air, you return from distant remembrance to appear to me: soul of the oasis where my life for an instant recovered contact with the forces of the cosmos. I see you again, Manuelita, your small face armed with the pugnacious winged brim of your hat, the rolled-up ostrich feather tossing heroically, your little steps full of suppressed impulses on the soil of heroic promises! Frail and nervous all of you is here before me. The powder sprinkled like snow on your face wasted by inner burning, your pink dresses that proclaim your virginity like a sunrise full of promise! And you astonishing flower of an heroic race, your magnetism when you bowed your head still draws me to you in spite of time! And yet Manuelita learn this if you can: *I was not thinking, I was not thinking of you: I have never thought of you.* At night in the deserted square when lovely clouds ran toward strange constellations, I under the sad electric light felt my infinite solitude. The grassland rose like a sea silvered in the background and residues from that sea—pitiable fierce men, unknown men shut in their somber will, their bloody stories suddenly forgotten that lived again unexpectedly in the night—wove about me the story of the young and fierce city, implacable conqueror, burning with the sharp fever of money and imme-

un'acre febbre di denaro e di gioie immediate. Io vi perdevo allora Manuelita, perdonate, tra la turba delle signorine elastiche dal viso molle inconsciamente feroce, violentemente eccitante tra le due bande di capelli lisci nell'immobilità delle dee della razza. Il silenzio era scandito dal trotto monotono di una pattuglia: e allora il mio anelito infrenabile andava lontano da voi, verso le calme oasi della sensibilità della vecchia Europa e mi si stringeva con violenza il cuore. Entravo, ricordo, allora nella biblioteca: io che non potevo Manuelita io che non sapevo pensare a voi. Le lampade elettriche oscillavano lentamente. Su da le pagine risuscitava un mondo defunto, sorgevano immagini antiche che oscillavano lentamente coll'ombra del paralume e sovra il mio capo gravava un cielo misterioso, gravido di forme vaghe, rotto a tratti da gemiti di melodramma: larve che si scioglievano mute per rinascere a vita inestinguibile nel silenzio pieno delle profondità meravigliose del destino. Dei ricordi perduti, delle immagini si componevano già morte mentre era più profondo il silenzio. Rivedo ancora Parigi, Place d'Italie, le baracche, i carrozzoni, i magri cavalieri dell'irreale, dal viso essiccato, dagli occhi perforanti di nostalgie feroci, tutta la grande piazza ardente di un concerto infernale stridente e irritante. Le bambine dei Bohémiens, i capelli sciolti, gli occhi arditi e profondi congelati in un languore ambiguo amaro attorno dello stagno liscio e deserto. E in fine Lei, dimentica, lontana, l'amore, il suo viso di zingara nell'onda dei suoni e delle luci che si colora di un incanto irreale: e noi in silenzio attorno allo stagno pieno di chiarori rossastri: e noi

diate delights. I lost you then Manuelita, pardon, in the crowd of mobile young women with soft faces unconsciously cruel, impetuously stimulating between two bands of glossy hair in the immobility of goddesses of your breed. Silence was measured by the monotonous trotting of a patrol: and then my unchecked breathing went far off from you toward the calm oases of the sensibility of old Europe and my heart bled wildly. I remember I then went into the library: I who could not, Manuelita, I who did not know how to think of you. The electric lamps swayed slowly. Up from the pages a dead world revived; old images that swayed slowly in the shadow of the lampshade arose, and over my head there weighed down a mysterious sky, pregnant with vague forms broken now and then by melodramatic wailing: ghosts that dissolved silently to be reborn to a life everlasting in the silence full of the wonderful profundity of destiny. Some lost recollections, some already defunct images took shape while silence was deepest. Again I saw Paris, Place d'Italie, the barracks, the caravans, the emaciated horsemen of unreality, their faces dried up, their eyes piercing with fierce nostalgia, the entire great square spirited with infernal strident irritating noise. The little girls of the Bohemians, their hair loose, their eyes fearless and intensely congealed in an ambiguous bitter faintness around the smooth and deserted pond. And after all She, oblivious, remote, her love, her Gypsy face in a wave of sounds and lights that makes unreal enchantment plausible; and we in silence around the pond full of reddish shimmering: and we still weary from a dream wandered at

ancora stanchi del sogno vagabondare a caso per quartieri ignoti fino a stenderci stanchi sul letto di una taverna lontana tra il soffio caldo del vizio noi là nell'incertezza e nel rimpianto colorando la nostra voluttà di riflessi irreali!

.   .   .   .

E così lontane da voi passavano quelle ore di sogno, ore di profondità mistiche e sensuali che scioglievano in tenerezze i grumi più acri del dolore, ore di felicità completa che aboliva il tempo e il mondo intero, lungo sorso alle sorgenti dell'Oblio! E vi rivedevo Manuelita poi: che vigilavate pallida e lontana: voi anima semplice chiusa nelle vostre semplici armi.

So Manuelita: voi cercavate la grande rivale. So: la cercavate nei miei occhi stanchi che mai non vi appresero nulla. Ma ora se lo potete sappiate: io dovevo restare fedele al mio destino: era un'anima inquieta quella di cui mi ricordavo sempre quando uscivo a sedermi sulle panchine della piazza deserta sotto le nubi in corsa. Essa era per cui solo il sogno mi era dolce. Essa era per cui io dimenticavo il vostro piccolo corpo convulso nella stretta del guanciale, il vostro piccolo corpo pericoloso tutto adorabile di snellezza e di forza. E pure vi giuro Manuelita io vi amavo vi amo e vi amerò sempre più di qualunque altra donna. . . . dei due mondi.

random in unknown places until we stretched out tired on a bed in some distant tavern, surrounded by the hot breath of vice, we there in uncertainty and regret coloring our voluptuousness of unreal reflections!

.   .   .   .

And so, away from you those hours of dream passed, hours of mystic and sensual profundity that dissolved in tenderness the most bitter swelling of grief, hours of complete happiness that abolished time and the whole world, a long drink at the springs of Oblivion! And then I saw you, Manuelita: how pallid and distant you kept watch: you simple soul hidden by your simple weapons.

I know, Manuelita: you searched for the great rival. I know: you searched for her in my tired eyes that never taught you a thing. But now if you can, learn this: I had to remain faithful to my fate: she was a restless soul whom I always remembered when I went out and sat on the benches of the deserted square under the running clouds. It was she who made dream my only sweetness. It was she who made me forget your fitful little body pressed into the pillow, your perilous little body wholly adorable for its slenderness and strength. And yet I swear to you Manuelita I loved you I love you and I will always love you more than any other woman. . . . in the two worlds.

SOGNO DI PRIGIONE

Nel viola della notte odo canzoni bronzee. La cella è bianca, il giaciglio è bianco. La cella è bianca, piena di un torrente di voci che muoiono nelle angeliche cune, delle voci angeliche bronzee è piena la cella bianca. Silenzio: il viola della notte: in rabeschi dalle sbarre bianche il blu del sonno. Penso ad Anika: stelle deserte sui monti nevosi: strade bianche deserte: poi chiese di marmo bianche: nelle strade Anika canta: un buffo dall'occhio infernale la guida, che grida. Ora il mio paese tra le montagne. Io al parapetto del cimitero davanti alla stazione che guardo il cammino nero delle macchine, su, giù. Non è ancor notte; silenzio occhiuto di fuoco: le macchine mangiano rimangiano il nero silenzio nel cammino della notte. Un treno: si sgonfia arriva in silenzio, è fermo: la porpora del treno morde la notte: dal parapetto del cimitero le occhiaie rosse che si gonfiano nella notte: poi tutto, mi pare, si muta in rombo: *Da un finestrino in fuga io? io ch'alzo le braccia nella luce!!* (il treno mi passa sotto rombando come un demonio).

DREAM IN PRISON

In the violet night I hear bronze *canzoni*. The cell is white, the pallet is white. The cell is white, full of a torrent of voices that die in the angelic cradles, the white cell is full of angelic bronze voices. Silence: the violet night: in arabesques of white bars the blue of sleep. I think of Anika: solitary stars on the snowy mountains: solitary white streets: then churches of white marble: in the streets Anika sings: shouting, a buffoon with an infernal eye guides her. Now my village between the mountains. I on the parapet of the cemetery before the station look at the black trail of engines, up, down. It is not yet night: silence sharp-eyed with fire: again and again the engines devour the black silence on the road of night. A train: gasps arrives in silence, stops: the purple of the train corrodes the night: from the parapet of the cemetery the red eye-sockets that swell in the night: then everything, it seems to me, changes to a roar. *From a car window I in flight? I who raise my arms in the light!* (rumbling like a daimon the train passes under me.)

LA GIORNATA DI UN NEVRASTENICO

(Bologna)

La vecchia città dotta e sacerdotale era avvolta di nebbie nel pomeriggio di dicembre. I colli trasparivano più lontani sulla pianura percossa di strepiti. Sulla linea ferroviaria si scorgeva vicino, in uno scorcio falso di luce plumbea lo scalo delle merci. Lungo la linea di circonvallazione passavano pomposamente sfumate figure femminili, avvolte in pelliccie, i capelli copiosamente romantici, avvicinandosi a piccole scosse automatiche, rialzando la gorgiera carnosa come volatili di bassa corte. Dei colpi sordi, dei fischi dallo scalo accentuavano la monotonia diffusa nell'aria. Il vapore delle macchine si confondeva colla nebbia: i fili si appendevano e si riappendevano ai grappoli di campanelle dei pali telegrafici che si susseguivano automaticamente.

Dalla breccia dei bastioni rossi corrosi nella nebbia si aprono silenziosamente le lunghe vie. Il malvagio vapore della nebbia intristisce tra i palazzi velando la cima delle torri, le lunghe vie silenziose deserte come dopo il saccheggio. Delle ragazze tutte piccole, tutte scure, artifiziosamente avvolte nella sciarpa traversano saltellando le vie, rendendole più vuote ancora. E nell'incubo della nebbia, in quel cimitero, esse mi sembrano a un tratto tanti piccoli animali, tutte uguali, saltellanti, tutte nere, che vadano a covare in un lungo letargo un loro malefico sogno.

THE DAY OF A NEUROTIC

The old and learned priestly city was enveloped in the fog of a December afternoon. The most distant hills were transparent on the flatland hammered by noise. Near the railroad the freight yard with merchandise could be seen in a false foreshortening of leaden light. Along the outer circle in shaded outline female figures wrapped in furs, their hair abundantly romantic, approached with small automatic jerks, pompously passed by, raising their fleshy wattles like courtyard hens. Dull thuds and whistles from the yard accentuated the monotony diffused in the air. The steam of the engines mixed with the fog: wires were continuously suspended from the clusters of belled insulators on the telegraph poles that automatically followed in sequence.

The long streets open silently in the breach of the red corroded bastions in the fog. The noxious vapor of the fog droops between the palaces, veiling the tops of the towers, the long silent streets deserted as if after pillaging. Girls quite small, quite dark, artfully wrapped in scarfs skip across the streets, leaving them still more empty. And in the incubus of fog, in that cemetery, they seem to me at that instant so many small animals, all identical, jumping, all black, going to hatch their pernicious dream in an extended lethargy.

Numerose le studentesse sotto i portici. Si vede subito che siamo in un centro di cultura. Guardano a volte coll'ingenuità di Ofelia, tre a tre, parlando a fior di labbra. Formano sotto i portici il corteo pallido e interessante delle grazie moderne, le mie colleghe, che vanno a lezione! Non hanno l'arduo sorriso d'Annunziano palpitante nella gola come le letterate, ma più raro un sorriso e più severo, intento e masticato, di prognosi riservata, le scienziate.

(Caffè) É passata la Russa. La piaga delle sue labbra ardeva nel suo viso pallido. È venuta ed è passata portando il fiore e la piaga delle sue labbra. Con un passo elegante, troppo semplice troppo conscio è passata. La neve seguita a cadere e si scioglie indifferente nel fango della via. La sartina e l'avvocato ridono e chiaccherano. I cocchieri imbacuccati tirano fuori la testa dal bavero come bestie stupite. Tutto mi è indifferente. Oggi risalta tutto il grigio monotono e sporco della città. Tutto fonde come la neve in questo pantano: e in fondo sento che è dolce questo dileguarsi di tutto quello che ci ha fatto soffrire. Tanto più dolce che presto la neve si stenderà ineluttabilmente in un lenzuolo bianco e allora potremo riposare in sogni bianchi ancora.

C'è uno specchio avanti a me e l'orologio batte: la luce mi giunge dai portici a traverso le cortine della vetrata. Prendo la penna: scrivo: cosa, non so: ho il sangue alle dita: scrivo: "l'amante nella penombra si aggraffia al viso dell'amante per scarnificare il suo sogno. . . ecc. ".

Numerous the coeds under the arcades. We see at once that we are in a cultural center. At times they look around with the ingenuousness of Ophelia, three talking to three, their lips barely moving. Under the arcades they form a pale and interesting procession of our modern Graces, my classmates who go to lectures! The girls in the sciences do not have the hard D'Annunzio smile, a throbbing in the throat like the girls in letters, but a smile more rare, more severe, earnest and thoughtful, prognoses reserved.

(Café) The Russian went by. The wound of her lips burned in her white face. She came and went, carrying the flower and wound of her lips. With an elegant step, too simple too conscious she went by. The snow continues to fall and dissolves indifferently in the muddy street. The little dressmaker and the lawyer laugh and chatter. Bundled up, the coachmen pull their heads up out of their coat collars like astonished beasts. I am indifferent to everything. Today the entire gray monotony of the dirty city is conspicuous. Everything melts like snow in this mess and deep down I feel how sweet is this dissolving of everything that has made us suffer. So much sweeter that soon the snow will spread ineluctably into a white sheet and then we can rest in white dreams once more.

Before me there is a mirror and the clock strikes: the light from the arcades reaches me through the curtains of the large window. I take my pen: I write: what, I don't know: blood pulsates at my fingertips: I write: "the lover in the dim light claws at the face of his beloved to lacerate his dream. . . etc."

(*Ancora per la via*) Tristezza acuta. Mi ferma il mio antico compagno di scuola, già allora bravissimo ed ora di già in belle lettere guercio professor purulento: mi tenta, mi confessa con un sorriso sempre più lercio. Conclude: potresti provare a mandare qualcosa all' "Amore Illustrato" (*Via*). Ecco inevitabile sotto i portici lo sciame aereoplanante delle signorine intellettuali, che ride e fa glu glu mostrando i denti, in caccia, sembra, di tutti i nemici della scienza e della cultura, che va a frangere ai piedi della cattedra. Già è l'ora! vado a infangarmi in mezzo alla via: l'ora che l'illustre somiero rampa con il suo carico di nera scienza catalogale   .   .   .   .

.   .   .   .   .

Sull'uscio di casa mi volgo e vedo il classico, baffuto, colossale emissario   .   .   .   .

Ah! i diritti della vecchiezza! Ah! quanti maramaldi!

(Notte) Davanti al fuoco lo specchio. Nella fantasmagoria profonda dello specchio i corpi ignudi avvicendano muti: e i corpi lassi e vinti nelle fiamme inestinte e mute, e come fuori del tempo i corpi bianchi stupiti inerti nella fornace opaca: bianca, dal mio spirito esausto silenziosa si sciolse, Eva si sciolse e mi risvegliò.

Passeggio sotto l'incubo dei portici. Una goccia di luce sanguina, poi l'ombra, poi una goccia di luce sanguigna, la dolcezza dei seppelliti. Scompaio in un vicolo ma dall'ombra

(Still along the street) Acute sadness. My old classmate stops me; once he was really the most clever and now he is indeed a squinting purulent teacher of belles-lettres: he tests me, professes to me with a smile ever filthier. Concludes: you should try to send something to "Love Illustrated." *(Street)* Here inevitably under the arcades, the swooping swarm of intellectual young women, who laugh and gobble gobble, showing their teeth, in pursuit it seems, of all the enemies of science and culture and who crash down at the feet of the professorial chair. Class time! I go to muddy myself in the middle of the street: now when the illustrious jackass climbs up with his cargo of black cataloguing science   .   .   .

.   .   .   .

At the door of the house I turn and see the classical mustache of the colossal emissary   .   .   .   .   .

Oh! The privileges of old age! How many betrayers!

(Night) In front of the fire the mirror. In the deep phantasmagoria of the mirror the naked and dumb bodies alternate: the weary and overcome bodies in flames extinct and dead: the inert astonished white bodies in the opaque furnace as if outside of time: from my exhausted spirit, white Eve silently freed herself and awakened me.

I pass under the incubus of the arcades. A drop of light bleeds, then shadow, then a drop of sanguine light, the sweetness of the buried. I disappear in an alley but from the shadow

sotto un lampione s'imbianca un'ombra che ha le labbra tinte. O Satana, tu che le troie notturne metti in fondo ai quadrivii, o tu che dall'ombra mostri l'infame cadavere di Ofelia, o Satana abbi pietà della mia lunga miseria!

under a street lamp a ghost that has painted lips whitens. O Satan, you who place whores nightly at street corners, O you who from the shadow show the infamous cadaver of Ophelia, O Satan, have pity on my enduring misery!

PASSEGGIATA IN TRAM IN AMERICA E RITORNO

Aspro preludio di sinfonia sorda, tremante violino a corda elettrizzata, tram che corre in una linea nel cielo ferreo di fili curvi mentre la mole bianca della città torreggia come un sogno, moltiplicato miraggio di enormi palazzi regali e barbari, i diademi elettrici spenti. Corro col preludio che tremola si assorda riprende si afforza e libero sgorga davanti al molo della piazza densa di navi e di carri. Gli alti cubi della città si sparpagliano tutti pel golfo in dadi infiniti di luce striati d'azzurro: nel mentre il mare tra le tanaglie del molo come un fiume che fugge tacito pieno di singhiozzi taciuti corre veloce verso l'eternità del mare che si balocca e complotta laggiù per rompere la linea dell'orizzonte.

Ma mi parve che la città scomparisse mentre che il mare rabbrividiva nella sua fuga veloce. Sulla poppa balzante io già ero portato lontano nel turbinare delle acque. Il molo, gli uomini erano scomparsi fusi come in una nebbia. Cresceva l'odore mostruoso del mare. La lanterna spenta s'alzava. Il gorgoglio dell'acqua tutto annegave irremissibilmente. Il battito forte nei fianchi del bastimento confondeva il battito del mio cuore e ne svegliava un vago dolore intorno come se stesse per aprirsi un bubbone. Ascoltavo il gorgoglio dell'acqua. L'acqua a volte mi pareva musicale, poi tutto ricadeva in un rombo e la terra e la luce mi erano strappate inconsciamente. Come amavo, ricordo,

ROUND TRIP: TROLLEY RIDE IN AMERICA

Harsh beginning of a muffled symphony, a violin quivering on an electric string, a trolley that runs in a line through a metallic sky of curved wires while the city's white massive structure towers like a dream, multiplied mirage of enormous regal and barbaric palaces, the electric diadems switched off. I race with the prelude that trembles deafens recovers invigorates itself and gushes before the jetty of the square crowded with ships and trucks. The cubic heights of the city are all scattered along the bay in infinite blocks of light striated blue: while the sea within the pincers of the breakwater, like a river that flies quietly full of stifled sobbing, runs swiftly toward the eternity of the ocean that trifles and plots down below to break the line of the horizon.

But it seemed to me the city disappeared when the sea shuddered in swift flight. On the bounding stern I was already carried far off in a whirl of waters. The jetty and the men had vanished, melted as in a mist. The abominable smell of the sea increased. The extinguished lamp lit up. Relentlessly the gurgling of the water drowned everything. The strong hammering against the sides of the ship mixed with my own heart-beat and awakened around it an uncertain soreness as if a bubo were about to burst. I listened to the gurgling of the water. At times the water seemed like music to me, then everything collapsed in a rumble and earth and light were unconsciously snatched from me. How

il tonfo sordo della prora che si sprofonda nell'onda che la raccoglie e la culla un brevissimo istante e la rigetta in alto leggera nel mentre il battello è una casa scossa dal terremoto che pencola terribilmente e fa un secondo sforzo contro il mare tenace e riattacca a concertare con i suoi alberi una certa melodia beffarda nell'aria, una melodia che non si ode, si indovina solo alle scosse di danza bizzarre che la scuotono!

C'erano due povere ragazze sulla poppa: "Leggera, siamo della leggera: te non la rivedi più la lanterna di Genova!" Eh! che importava in fondo! Ballasse il bastimento, ballasse fino a Buenos-Aires: questo dava allegria: e il mare se la rideva con noi del suo riso così buffo e sornione! Non so se fosse la bestialità irritante del mare, il disgusto che quel grosso bestione col suo riso mi dava . . . basta: i giorni passavano. Tra i sacchi di patate avevo scoperto un rifugio. Gli ultimi raggi rossi del tramonto che illuminavano la costa deserta! costeggiavamo da un giorno. Bellezza semplice di tristezza maschia. Oppure a volte quando l'acqua saliva ai finestrini io seguivo il tramonto equatoriale sul mare. Volavano uccelli lontano dal nido ed io pure: ma senza gioia. Poi sdraiato in coperta restavo a guardare gli alberi dondolare nella notte tiepida in mezzo al rumore dell'acqua. . . .

Riodo il preludio scordato delle rozze corde sotto l'arco di violino del tram domenicale. I piccoli dadi bianchi sorridono sulla costa tutti in cerchio come una dentiera enorme tra il fetido odore di catrame e di carbone misto al nauseante odor d'infinito. Fumano i vapori agli scali desolati.

I loved, I remember, the muffled splash of the prow that sinks into the wave that gathers it in and rocks it for the briefest instant and throws it lightly upward while the ship is a house shaken by an earthquake that totters terribly and exerts itself against the unyielding sea and again attacks in concert with its masts a certain mocking melody in the air, a melody that is not heard and only imagined because of the tremors of the fantastic dance that shake it!

There were two poor girls on the stern: "Broke, we are penniless: you will never see Genoa's lighthouse again." Well, what did it matter in the end! Let the ship dance, dance as far as Buenos Aires: this cheered us: and the sea itself laughed with us, its laughter so comic and surly! I do not know if it was the galling bestiality of the sea, the disgust that big strong monster provoked in me with its laughter . . . enough: the days passed. Among the sacks of potatoes, I had discovered a refuge. How the last rays of sunset brightened the deserted coast! We hugged the coastline for a day. Simple beauty of manly sadness. Or at times when the water leaped to the portholes, I followed the equatorial sunset on the sea. Birds flew far from their nests and I too: but without joy. Then I stretched out and remained on deck to watch the masts sway in the warm night in the middle of the sounding water. . . .

I hear again the discordant prelude of crude strings under the violin bow of the Sunday trolley. The little white cubes all in a circle on the shore smile like an enormous denture between the fetid smell of tar and coal mixed with the sickening smell of infinity. At the lonely docks the steamers

Domenica. Per il porto pieno di carcasse delle lente file umane, formiche dell'enorme ossario. Nel mentre tra le tanaglie del molo rabbrividisce un fiume che fugge, tacito pieno di singhiozzi taciuti fugge veloce verso l'eternità del mare, che si balocca e complotta laggiù per rompere la linea dell'orizzonte.

have their smoke up. Sunday. In the port full of carcasses in drawn-out human rows, ants in an enormous charnel house. While within the pincers of the breakwater there shudders a river that flies quietly full of stifled sobbing, flies swiftly toward the eternity of the ocean that trifles and plots down below to break the line of the horizon.

GENOVA

Poi che la nube si fermò nei cieli
Lontano sulla tacita infinita
Marina chiusa nei lontani veli,
E ritornava l'anima partita
Che tutto a lei d'intorno era già arcana-
mente illustrato del giardino il verde
Sogno nell'apparenza sovrumana
De le corrusche sue statue superbe:
E udìi canto udìi voce di poeti
Ne le fonti e le sfingi sui frontoni
Benigne un primo oblìo parvero ai proni
Umani ancor largire: dai segreti
Dedali uscìi: sorgeva un torreggiare
Bianco nell'aria: innumeri dal mare
Parvero i bianchi sogni dei mattini
Lontano dileguando incatenare
Come un ignoto turbine di suono.
Tra le vele di spuma udivo il suono.
Pieno era il sole di Maggio.

§

Sotto la torre orientale, ne le terrazze verdi ne la lavagna
        cinerea
Dilaga la piazza al mare che addensa le navi inesausto
Ride l'arcato palazzo rosso dal portico grande:

58

GENOA

After the cloud paused in the sky
Far-off on the silent infinite
Seacoast enclosed by remote veils
The departed spirit returned
When everything about it was a green dream
Of the garden already arcanely
illuminated in the superhuman appearance
Of the flashing magnificent statues:
And I heard song I heard the speech of poets
In the fountains and on the pediments
The benign sphinxes still seemed to grant
A first forgetfulness to prone humanity: I emerged
From secret labyrinths: a white tower
Arose in the air: from the sea the innumerable
White dreams of morning seemed
In the distance to scatter their shackles
Like a strange turbine of sound.
Between the sails of spume I heard the sound.
The May sun was at its height.

§

Under the oriental tower, in the green terraces on the
       ashen slate
The square floods to the inexhaustible sea that amasses ships
The red arched palace laughs through its great portico:

Come le cateratte del Niagara
Canta, ride, svaria ferrea la sinfonia feconda urgente al
    mare:
Genova canta il tuo canto!
Entro una grotta di porcellana
Sorbendo caffè
Guardavo dall'invetriata la folla salire veloce
Tra le venditrici uguali a statue, porgenti
Frutti di mare con rauche grida cadenti
Su la bilancia immota:
Così ti ricordo ancora e ti rivedo imperiale
Su per l'erta tumultuante
Verso la porta disserrata
Contro l'azzurro serale,
Fantastica di trofei
Mitici tra torri nude al sereno,
A te aggrappata d'intorno
La febbre de la vita
Pristina: e per i vichi lubrici di fanali il canto
Instornellato de le prostitute
E dal fondo il vento del mar senza posa.

§

Per i vichi marini nell'ambigua
Sera cacciava il vento tra i fanali
Preludii dal groviglio delle navi:
I palazzi marini avevan bianchi

Like Niagara Falls
The fecund urgent symphony inexorably sings, laughs,
      swerves to the sea:
Genoa sing your song!
Inside a porcelain grotto
Sipping coffee
I watched through the window the crowd
Rush by the pedlars, like statues offering
Shellfish, their raucous cries falling
On the fixed scales:
So I still remember you and I see you
Imperial on the uproarious hilt
Toward the open gateway
Against the evening blue
Fantastic with mythic
Trophies between the bare towers in the sky,
The fever of pristine life
Anchored about you:
And through the indecent alleys of street lamps
The folk song of the prostitutes
And from down below the sea's wind unceasingly.

§

Through the marine alleys in the ambiguous
Evening between the street lamps the wind hunted
Preludes from the tangle of ships:
The marine palaces were white arabesques

Arabeschi nell'ombra illanguidita
Ed andavamo io e la sera ambigua:
Ed io gli occhi alzavo su ai mille
E mille e mille occhi benevoli
Delle Chimere nei cieli: .   .   .   .   .   .
Quando,
Melodiosamente
D'alto sale, il vento come bianca finse una visione di
      Grazia
Come dalla vicenda infaticabile
De le nuvole e de te stelle dentro del cielo serale
Dentro il vico marino in alto sale,   .   .   .
Dentro il vico ché rosse in alto sale
Marino l'ali rosse dei fanali
Rabescavano l'ombra illanguidita,   .   .   .
Che nel vico marino, in alto sale
Che bianca e lieve e querula salì!
"Come nell' ali rosse dei fanali
Bianca e rossa nell'ombra del fanale
Che bianca e lieve e tremula salì: . . ."
Ora di già nel rosso del fanale
Era già l'ombra faticosamente
Bianca   .   .   .   .
Bianca quando nel rosso del fanale
Bianca lontana faticosamente
L'eco attonita rise un irreale
Riso: e che l'eco faticosamente
E bianca e lieve e attonita salì . . .

In the drooping shadow
And we started off the ambiguous evening, and I:
I raised my eyes to the thousand
And thousand and thousand benevolent
Eyes of the Chimeras in the skies:
When
Melodiously
From a salty height the wind simulated a white vision of
　　　Grace
As of untiring change
Of clouds and stars within the evening sky
Within the marine alley at a salty height,
Within the marine alley that reddened at a salty height
The red wings of the street lamps
Adorned the drooping shadow with arabesques
That in the marine alley at a salty height
That white and light and querulous it arose!
"As in the red wings of the street lamps
White and red in the shadow of the street lamp
That white and light and quivering it arose: . . ."
Even now in the red of the street lamp
The shadow was already tediously
White
White when in the red of the street lamp
White distant tediously
The astonished echo laughed an unreal
Laugh: for the white and light astonished echo
Tediously arose . . .

Di già tutto d'intorno
Lucea la sera ambigua:
Battevano i fanali
Il palpito nell'ombra.
Rumori lontano franavano
Dentro silenzii solenni
Chiedendo: se dal mare
Il riso non saliva . . .
Chiedendo se l'udiva
Infaticabilmente
La sera: a la vicenda
Di nuvole là in alto
Dentro del cielo stellare.

§

Al porto il battello si posa
Nel crepuscolo che brilla
Negli alberi quieti di frutti di luce,
Nel paesaggio mitico
Di navi nel seno dell'infinito
Ne la sera
Calida di felicità, lucente
In un grande in un grande velario
Di diamanti disteso sul crepuscolo,
In mille e mille diamanti in un grande velario vivente
Il battello si scarica
Ininterrottamente cigolante,

Already all around
The ambiguous evening glittered:
The street lamps pulsated
In the shadow.
Distant noises crumbled
Within solemn silences
Asking: if laughter
Was not rising from the sea . . .
Asking if the evening
Unwearyingly
Heard it: in the shifting
Of clouds there up above
Within the starlit sky.

§

At the port the ship lies
In the dusk that glistens
Through the masts quiet with fruits of light,
In the mythic landscape
Of ships on the breast of the infinite
In the evening
Warm with felicity, luminous
In a great in a great curtain
Of diamonds spread on the twilight,
Diamonds by the thousands in a great living curtain
The ship unloads
Uninterruptedly creaking

Instancabilemente introna
E la bandiera è calata e il mare e il cielo
    è d'oro e sul molo
Corrono i fanciulli e gridano
Con gridi di felicità.
Già a frotte s'avventurano
I viaggiatori alla città tonante
Che stende le sue piazze e le sue vie:
La grande luce mediterranea
S'è fusa in pietra di cenere:
Pei vichi antichi e profondi
Fragore di vita, gioia intensa e fugace:
Velario d'oro di felicità
È il cielo ove il sole ricchissimo
Lasciò le sue spoglie preziose

E la Città comprende
E s'accende
E la fiamma titilla ed assorbe
I resti magnifici del sole,
E intesse un sudario d'oblìo
Divino per gli uomini stanchi.
Perdute nel crepuscolo tonante
Ombre di viaggiatori
Vanno per la Superba
Terribili e grotteschi come i ciechi.

Untiringly deafens
And the flag is lowered and the sea and the sky are golden
        and on the jetty
The children run and scream
Their cries of happiness.
Now the travelers venture in groups
Into the thundering city
Reaching into the squares and streets:
The great Mediterranean light
Is fused in ashen stone:
Through the old and deep alleys
Roar of life, intense and fugitive joy:
The sky where the most magnificent sun
Left its precious spoil
Is a golden curtain of happiness

And The City is aware
And lights up
And the flame titillates and swallows up
The magnificent residues of the sun
And interweaves a shroud of oblivion
Divine for tired men.
Lost in the thundering twilight
Shadows of travelers
Fearful and grotesque as the blind
Walk through La Superba.

§

Vasto, dentro un odor tenue vanito
Di catrame, vegliato da le lune
Elettriche, sul mare appena vivo
Il vasto porto si addorme.
S'alza la nube delle ciminiere
Mentre il porto in un dolce scricchiolìo
Dei cordami s'addorme: e che la forza
Dorme, dorme che culla la tristezza
Inconscia de le cose che saranno
E il vasto porto oscilla dentro un ritmo
Affaticato e si sente
La nube che si forma dal vomito silente.

§

O Siciliana proterva opulente matrona
A le finestre ventose del vico marinaro
Nel seno della città percossa di suoni di navi e di
        carri
Classica mediterranea femina dei porti:
Pei grigi rosei della città di ardesia
Sonavano i clamori vespertini
E poi più quieti i rumori dentro la notte serena:
Vedevo alle finestre lucenti come le stelle
Passare le ombre de la famiglie marine: e canti
Udivo lenti ed ambigui ne le vene de la
        città mediterranea:

§

Vast within a slight disappearing odor
Of tar, watched over by electric
Moons, the vast port sleeps
On the barely moving sea.
A haze rises from the funnels
While the port sleeps
In a gentle creaking of cordage: and when strength
Sleeps, sleeps as it lulls sadness
Unaware of things that will be
The vast port vibrates within a weary
Rhythm and there is an awareness
The haze is shaped by the silent vomiting.

§

O fleshy brazen Sicilian matron
At the windy window of the maritime alley
In the heart of the city hammered by sounds of ships and
    trucks
Classic Mediterranean female of the ports:
The outcries at evening resounded
Through the gray pink of the slate city
And then the noises were quieter in the serene night:
In the shining windows bright like stars I saw
The shadow of seamen's families pass by: and I heard
Songs slow and ambiguous in the veins of the
    Mediterranean city:

Ch'era la notte fonda.
Mentre tu siciliana, dai cavi
Vetri in un torvo giuoco
L'ombra cava e la luce vacillante
O siciliana, ai capezzoli
L'ombra rinchiusa tu eri
La Piovra de le notti mediterranee.
Cigolava cigolava cigolava di catene
La gru sul porto nel cavo de la notte serena:
E dentro il cavo de la notte serena
E nelle braccia di ferro
Il debole cuore batteva un più alto palpito: tu
La finestra avevi spenta:
Nuda mistica in alto cava
Infinitamente occhiuta devastazione era la notte
        tirrena.

It was a deep night.
While you, O Sicilian, from the hollow window panes
In a grim interplay
Of concave shadow and vacillating light
Were enclosed up to the nipples
In shadow, O Sicilian,
The Octopus of Mediterranean nights.
The crane on the wharf in the hollow of the serene night
Creaked creaked creaked in its chains:
And in the hollow of the serene night
And in its iron arms
The weak heart beat a louder throb: you
Had darkened the window:
Mystical nude in high hollow
The Tyrrhenian night was a devastation of innumerable
    eyes.

[FRAMMENTO]

L'albero oscilla a tocchi nel silenzio.
Una tenue luce bianca e verde cade dall'albero.
Il cielo limpido all'orizzonte, carico verde e dorato dopo
      la burrasca.
Il quadro bianco della lanterna in alto
Illumina il segreto notturno: dalla finestra
Le corde dall'alto a triangolo d'oro
E un globo bianco di fumo
Che non esiste come musica
Sopra del cerchio coi tocchi dell'acqua in sordina.

SHIP ON ITS WAY

Now and then the mast sways in the silence.
A slender white and green light falls from the mast.
Bright the sky on the horizon, deep green and golden after
      the storm.
Up high the white square of the lantern
Illuminates the night's secret: from the window above
Ropes in a gold triangle
And a globe white with smoke
That exists not as music
Above the circle with the pulsing of water, muted.

They were all torn
and cover'd with
the boy's
blood

POEMS
AND
FRAGMENTS

NOTTURNO TEPPISTA

Firenze nel fondo era gorgo di luci di fremiti
      sordi:
Con ali di fuoco i lunghi rumori fuggenti
Del tram spaziavano: il fiume mostruoso
Torpido riluceva come un serpente a squame.
Su un circolo incerto le inquiete facce beffarde
Dei ladri, ed io tra i doppi lunghi
      cipressi uguali a fiaccole spente
Più aspro ai cipressi le siepi
Più aspro del fremer dei bussi,
Che dal mio cuore il mio amore,
Che dal mio cuore, l'amore un ruffiano che intonò e cantò:
Amo le vecchie troie
Gonfie lievitate di sperma
Che cadono come rospi a quattro zampe sovra la
      coltrice rossa
E aspettano e sbuffano ed ansimano
Flaccide come mantici.

HOODLUM AT NIGHT

Florence down below was a whirlpool of lights, trembling
      dully:
On wings of fire the tedious vanishing noises
Of the street car soared: the huge sluggish
River glittered like a scaly serpent.
Above a wavering circle the restless mocking faces
Of the thieves, and I between a long double row of
      uniform cypresses like wasted torches,
Harsher than hedges to the cypresses
Harsher than quivering box-trees,
As from my heart my love
As from my heart, love a pimp intoned and sang:
I love the old whores
Swollen with ferment of sperm
Who fall like toads on four paws on the
      red featherbed
And wait and pant and snort
Flaccid like bellows.

IL TEMPO MISERABILE CONSUMI

Il tempo miserabile consumi
Me, la mia gioia e tutta la speranza
Venga la morte pallida e mi dica
Pàrtiti figlio.
Un dopopranzo, sdraiato sull'erba
Pieno di cibi e di languore, anch'io
Alla donna insaziata e battagliera,
E ben lontana,
Avrei fatto dei versi deliziosi:
Mi rose e avvelenò fin dall'infanzia
Una cucina perfida e nefanda
Il gusto fine.
La morte magra e seria ha nella voce
Un'armonia che pure io gusto tutta
Ma il mondo grasso l'ha scomunicata
E la disprezza
I ricchi son potenti al giorno d'oggi
Fanno le leggi e decretan la fame
Ai poveretti che cercan nel mondo
Un ideale
L'ideale emaciato e affievolito
Va con occhi infantili ed incosciente
Vende [. . .]
Pei lupanari
Per non toccarlo s'alzan la sottana

OPPRESSIVE TIME

May this oppressive time destroy me,
Me, my joy and all my hope
May pallid death come and say to me
Come on son.
After lunch full of food and sluggish
Stretched out on the grass, even I
I should have made delightful verses
To the unsatisfied pugnacious
Woman far enough away:
A nasty and foul cuisine
Gnawed at me
And poisoned my sensitive taste from childhood.
Lean and grave death has in its voice
A harmony I still taste fully
But the fat world has excommunicated it
And scorns it
The rich are powerful these days
They make the laws and decree hunger
For the poor who search in the world
An ideal
The emaciated and weakened ideal
Goes with infantile and unconscious eyes
Sells [. . .]
Through brothels
For not touching it the women

Le donne. I bruti ànno viotato l'ora
Sacra che passa e che darà un domani
Fulgido enorme
I frenetici i pazzi su dal suolo
Nascono come funghi dopo pioggia
E ai loro tuoni di teatro buffo
Rispondono profondi
I gravi rospi e le ranocchie tenere

In melopea, dal lume della luna
Madreperlacea sopra la putredine
Inebriati
O Morte o morte vecchio capitano
Ischeletrito stendi le falcate
Braccia e portami in stretta disperata
Verso le stelle
O muto e cieco reduce, tra il marmo
Delle tue braccia suoni la mia testa
Eletrizzata esausta come corda
Che si dirompe

Raise their skirts. The brutes have violated the holy
Hour that passes and that will grant a tomorrow
Dazzling and immense
The frenetic the crazy spring up
From the soil like mushrooms after a rain
And to their comic stage-roars
The solemn toads and the tender frogs
Enraptured

Respond deeply in accompaniment
By the light of the moon
Nacreous over the drunken putrefaction
O Death O death old captain
Reduced to a skeleton extend your arms
Like scythes and carry me in a desperate embrace
Toward the stars
O blind and silent veteran between the marble
Of your arms may my head ring
Electrified worn out like a string
That snaps

SPADA BARBARICA

Voi che rompete le onde della sera
Colla punta del piede, in sul balcone

. . . .

O se avessi sirena
Una sol goccia del vostro sudore
Sulla lingua ardente, una sol goccia.
Ma la vostra fronte marmorea
Ma il vostro taglio scarlatto
Mi irridono metallici
Vergine inaccessibile una goccia. . .

. . . .

Idolo, nel mio sangue di cristiano
Io sento la vertigine colare
Idolo, il fuoco della distruzione
Mi prende. Sulla vostra testa mozza
Idolo il vostro sangue pagano
Paradisiaco sangue io beverò
Il vostro sangue magnifico e aborrito
Il vostro sangue dolce e soffocante
Il vostro sangue che odora di muschio
Il vostro sangue tappeto regale
Dove si smorza il passo della vita
Gocciolerà lampeggiante
Stilla di verità eterna
Clessidra degli eroi e degli dei.

BARBARIC SWORD

You who break the waves of evening
With the tip of your toe on the balcony
.   .   .   .

O if I had, siren,
Only a drop of your sweat
On my thirsty tongue, only a drop.
But your marble brow
But your scarlet slash
Deride me with their hardness
Inaccessible virgin, a drop. . . .
.   .   .   .

Idol, I feel the dizziness drip
Into my Christian blood
Idol, the fire of destruction
Seizes me. On your lopped-off head
Idol I will drink
Your pagan paradisiacal blood
Your magnificent and detested blood
Your sweet and choking blood
Your blood that smells of moss
Your blood a regal carpet
Where life's step grows faint
A drop of eternal truth
Will drip flashing
Clepsydra of heroes and of gods.

Ho una lama lucente
Che vince lo splendore dei vostri occhi,
Che fredda vorace vuol spegnere
Il suo splendore nella gola vostra
E ritornarsene vittoriosa
Di un trofeo di rossi diamanti
Di rossi diamanti che corrono
Su per il filo terribile folgoranti
E passano come meteora
E cadono silenziosamente
Nel grembo della terra genitrice
Oh che il tuo corpo mi versi
O donna le sue primavere
Più dolci in un fiotto che grava
Lambente i miei piedi severi
Con un tardo singhiozzo soffocato
Con un tardo singhiozzo soffocato:
Ed io camminerò sopra il tappeto
Rosso e movente, come un re in esilio
In un sogno di regno sopra i cieli.

I have a bright flashing blade
Brighter than the splendor of your eyes
That voracious and cold wishes to quench
Its splendor on your throat
And to return victorious
With a trophy of red diamonds
Of red diamonds that run
Dazzling along a terrible thread
And pass like meteors
And fall noiselessly
On the lap of Mother Earth
O may your body spill out to me
O woman your springtime
More sweet in a gush that oppresses
Lapping my impassive feet
With a slow suffocated sob
With a slow suffocated sob:
And I will walk over the red
Moving carpet like a king in exile
Dreaming of a realm over the skies.

UNA STRANA ZINGARELLA

Tu sentirai le rime scivolare
In cadenza nel caldo della stanza
Sopra al guanciale pallida a sognare
Ti volgerai, di questa lenta danza
Magnetica il sussurro a respirare.
La luna stanca è andata a riposare
Gli ulivi taccion, solo un ubriaco
Che si stanca a cantare e ricantare:
Tu magra e sola con i tuoi capelli
Sei restata. Nel cielo a respirare
Stanno i tuoi sogni. Volgiti ed ascolta
Nella notte gelata il mio cantare
Sulle tue spalle magroline e gialle
I capelli vorrei veder danzare
Sei pura come il suone e senza odore
Un tuo bacio è acerbetto e sorridente
E doloroso—e l'occhio è rilucente
È troppo bello, l'occhio è perditore.
Sicuramente tu non sai cantare
Ma la vocetta deve essere acuta
E perforante come il violino
E sorridendo deve pizzicare
Il cuore. I tuoi capelli sulle spalluccine?
Ami i profumi? E perché vai vestita
Di sangue? Ami le chiese?
No tu temi i profumi. Il corpicino

A STRANGE LITTLE GYPSY

You will hear the rhymes slide
In cadence in the warmth of the room
Pale, you will turn on the cushion
To dream and breathe the whisper
Of this slow magnetic dance.
The tired moon has gone to rest
The olive trees are silent except for a drunkard
Who tires himself singing and singing:
Slender and alone, you and your hair
Are left. Your dreams are breathing
In the sky. Turn and listen
In the frosty night to my song
I would like to see your hair dance
On your slender yellow shoulders
You are clean as sound and do not smell
Your kiss is slightly bitter pleasing
Painful — your eye is glittering
Is too beautiful, your eye damns me.
Surely you do not know how to sing
But your small voice must be sharp
And piercing as the violin
And pleasing it must pluck
The heart. Your hair on your small shoulders?
Do you love perfume? And why are you dressed
In blood? Do you love churches?
No you are afraid of perfume. Your small body

È troppo fine e gli occhi troppo neri
Oh se potessi vederti agitare
La tua animuccia tagliente tremare
E i tuoi occhi lucenti arrotondare
Mentre il santo linfatico e canoro
Che dovevi tentare
Spande in ginocchio nuvole d'incenso
Ringraziando il Signore
E non lo puoi amare
Christus vicisti
L'avorio del crocifisso
Vince l'avorio del tuo ventre
Dalla corona non sì dolce e gloriosa
Nera increspata movente
Nell'ombra grigia vertiginosa
E tu piangi in ginocchio per terra colle mani sugli occhi
E i tuoi piedi lunghi e brutti
Allargati per terra come zampe
D'una bestia ribelle e mostruosa.
Che sapore avranno le tue lacrimucce?
Un poco di fuoco? Io vorrei farne
Un diadema fantastico e portarlo
Sul mio capo nell'ora della morte
Per udirmi parlare in confidenza
I demonietti dai piedi forcuti.
Povera bimba come ti calunnio
Perché hai i capelli tragici
E ti vesti di rosso e non odori.

Is too slender and your eyes too black
Oh if you could see yourself shaking
Your small caustic spirit trembling
And your shining eyes rounded
While the lympathic and melodious saint
Whom you had to entice
Spills clouds of incense on his knees
Thanking the Lord
And you cannot love him
Christus vicisti
The ivory of the crucifix
Overcomes the ivory of your belly
And its crown not so sweet and proud
Black curled moving
In the gray dizzy shadow
And you weep knees to the ground hands over your eyes
Your long and ugly feet
Spread on the ground like the paws
Of a rebellious and monstrous beast.
What taste will your worthless tears have?
A little fire? I would like to make
A fantastic diadem and wear it
On my head at the hour of my death
To hear the little demons with forked feet
Speak to me in confidence.
Poor child how I slander you
Because you have tragic hair
And you dress in red and do not smell.

TRE GIOVANI FIORENTINE CAMMINANO

Ondulava sul passo verginale
Ondulava la chioma musicale
Nello splendore del tiepido sole
Eran tre vergini e una grazia sola
Ondulava sul passo verginale.
Crespa e nera la chioma musicale
Eran tre vergini e una grazia sola
E sei piedini in marcia militare.

THREE FLORENTINE GIRLS WALK

Rolled with a virginal gait
Rolled, head of hair like music
In the splendor of the warm sun
There were three girls all of one grace
Rolled with a virginal gait
Curly black head of hair like music
There were three girls all of one grace
And six little feet in a marche militaire.

OSCAR WILDE A S. MINIATO

O città fantastica piena di suoni sordi . . .
Mentre sulle scalee lontano io salivo davanti
A te infuocata in linee lambenti di fuoco
Nella sera gravida, tra i cipressi.
Salivo con un'amica giovane grave
Che sacrificava dai primi anni
All'amore malinconico e suicida dell'uomo:
Ridevano giù per le scale
Ragazzi accaniti briachi di beffa
Sopra un circolo attorno ad un soldo invisibile.
Il fiume mostruoso luceva torpido come un serpente a
        squame;
Salivamo, essa oppressa e anelante,
Io cogli occhi rivolti alla funebre febbre incendiaria
Che bruciava te, o nero naviglio alberato di torri
Nell'ultime febbri dei tempi remoti o città:
Odore amaro d'alloro ventava sordo dall'alto
Attorno al bianco chiostro sepolcrale:
Ma bella come te, battello bruciato tra l'alto
Soffio glorioso del ricordo, gridai o città,
O sogno sublime di tendere in fiamme
I corpi alla chimera non saziata
Amarissimo brivido funebre davanti all'incendio sordo
        lunare.

92

OSCAR WILDE AT SAN MINIATO

O fantastic city full of dull sounds . . .
I was climbing up the great stairway in sight of you
Far-off aflame with lambent lines of fire
Among the cypresses that pregnant evening.
I was climbing up with a young thoughtful friend
Who from her first years had sacrificed herself
To the melancholy and suicidal love for a man:
Down along the stairs in a circle around an invisible
Penny, boys in a drunken frenzy
Laughed at their own fun-making.
The monstrous torpid river shone like a scaly
        serpent;
We climbed up, she oppressed and gasping,
I, my eyes turned back to the mournful feverish fire
That set you ablaze, O dark ship with towers like masts
In the final fever of ages removed, O city:
Bitter odor of laurel blew dully from the height
Around the white sepulchral cloister:
But beautiful as you, ship burnt in the high
Glorious breath of remembrance, I screamed, O city,
O sublime dream of giving
To the unsatiated chimera bodies in flame—
Most bitter funereal shudder before the insensible lunar
        blaze

FIRENZE CICISBEA

Scampanava la Pasqua per la via
Calzaioli, le donne erano liete
Quel giorno ed innocenti le fanciulle
Di sotto ai cappelloni ultima moda.
E ingiovanito mi sembrava il duomo . . .
Ed i piedini andavano armoniosi
Portando i cappelloni battaglieri
Che armavano di un'ala gli occhi fieri
Del lor languore solo, nel bel giorno.
Il cannone tuonò ma non riscosse
Le signorine che andavano a messa
E continuava il calmo cicaleggio.
Una colomba si librava molle.

FATUOUS FLORENCE

Easter bells pealed on the Via
Calzaioli. The women were joyful
That day and the girls innocent
Under their hats in the latest fashion.
And the duomo seemed to me made young again . . .
And little feet walked by harmoniously,
Girls wearing their warlike wide-brimmed hats
That armed with a wing their eyes
Proud of their languor that lovely day.
The cannon thundered but did not startle
The girls as they walked to Mass
And continued their calm chattering.
A dove hovered softly.

FIRENZE VECCHIA

Ho visto il tuo palazzo palpitare
Di mille fiamme in una sera calda
O Firenze, il magnifico palazzo.
Già la folla à riempito la gran piazza
E vocia verso il suo palazzo vecchio
E beve la sua anima maliarda.
La confraternita di buona morte
Porta una bara sotto le tue mura:
Questo m'allieta questo m'assicura
Della tua forza di contro alla morte:
Non bruciano le tue ferree midolla
I tempi nuovi e non l'amaro agreste
Delle tue genti: in ricordanze in feste
L'àspero sangue sotto a te ribolla.
O ferro o sangue o fiamma è tutto fuoco
Che brucia la viltà dentro le vene!
A te dai petti e dalle gole piene,
Di gioia e forza un'inesausta polla!

OLD FLORENCE

I have seen your palace pulsate
With a thousand flames on a warm evening,
O Florence, your magnificent palace.
Already the crowd has filled the great square
And bawls against the old palace
And drinks its wizard spirit.
The brotherhood of proper death
Carries a bier under your walls:
This delights me this assures me
Of your strength against death:
The new times do not burn your iron marrow
Nor the rustic bitterness
Of your people: in remembering feasts
The harsh blood may boil under you again.
Iron or blood or flame is all one fire
That burns cowardice within the vein!
To you from breasts and full throats
An inexhaustible spring of joy and strength!

BOBOLI

Nel giardino spettrale
Dove il lauro reciso
Spande spoglie ghirlande sul passato,
Nella sera autunnale,
Io lento vinto e solo
Ho il profumo tuo biondo rievocato.
Dalle aride pendici
Aspre, arrossate ne l'ultimo sole
Giungevano i rumori
Rauchi già di una lontana vita.
Io su le spoglie aiuole
Io t'invocavo: o quali le tue voci
Ultimo furon, quale il tuo profumo
Più caro, quale il sogno più inquieto
Quale il vertiginoso appassionato
Ribelle sguardo d'oro?
Si udiva una fanfara
Straziante salire; il fiume in piena
Portava silenzioso
I riflessi dei fasti d'altri tempi.
Io mi affaccio a un balcone
E mi investe suadente
Tenero e grandioso
Fondo e amaro il profumo dell'alloro:
Ed ella mi è presente
(Tra le statue spettrali nel tramonto.)

BOBOLI

In the spectral garden
Where the cut laurel
Scatters bare garlands on the past,
In the autumnal evening
Overcome and alone
I slowly conjured up again your blonde perfume.
Raucous outcries from life at a distance
Came naturally
Off the harsh barren
Reddened hillsides in the dying sun.
I over your bare flowerbeds
I invoked you: O which of your voices
Was final? Which perfume dearer?
Which dream more disturbed?
Which rebellious golden glance
Impassionately dizzy?
A piercing fanfare was heard
Rising: the silent river
In full tide carried
The reflections of the splendor of other times.
I appear on a balcony
And the tender and magnificent
Deep and bitter perfume of laurel
Overwhelms me persuasively:
And she is here with me
(Among the spectral statues at sunset.)

SONETTO PERFIDO E FOCOSO

Io voglio nel sonetto pastorale
Te luccicante nelle bionde anelle
Te dal nascente tuo sesso ribelle
Inasperita, nuda incatenare;

E con sacro fervore esagitare
L'aroma acerbo delle membra snelle
E piamente sopra la tua pelle
Lunghi e superbi [. . . .] rievocare:

Per veder gli occhi tuoi torbidi e verdi
Che accese l'angiol che ti dorme accanto
A notte tarda nei sogni infiniti

Dal profondo implorarmi, mentre un tardo
Sospiro apra la bocca mortuaria
Al riso bianco dei denti immortale.

EVIL AND IMPETUOUS SONNET

In a pastoral sonnet it is you I want
Glittering with blonde ringlets
To enchain you, naked, embittered
From the dawning of your rebellious sex;

And to excite with consecrated fervor
The unripe scent of your slender limbs
And to evoke piously over your flesh
Long and wonderful. [. . . .]

In order to see your turbid and green
Eyes that your angel who sleeps beside you lit
Late into the night in endless dreams

From the depths pray for me while a late
Sigh may open the mortuary mouth
To the white laughter of your immortal teeth.

POESIA FACILE

Pace non cerco, guerra non sopporto
Tranquillo e solo vo pel mondo in sogno
Pieno di canti soffocati. Agogno
La nebbia ed il silenzio in un gran porto.

In un gran porto pien di vele lievi
Pronte a salpar per l'orizzonte azzurro
Dolci ondulando, mentre che il sussurro
Del vento passa con accordi brevi.

E quegli accordi il vento se li porta
Lontani sopra il mare sconosciuto.
Sogno. La vita è triste ed io son solo

O quando o quando in un mattino ardente
L'anima mia si sveglierà nel sole
Nel sole eterno, libera e fremente.

JUST A POEM

I do not seek peace. I cannot endure war
Quiet and alone I go through the world in a dream
Full of suppressed songs. I hanker for
The mist and silence in a great harbor.

In a great harbor full of soft sails
Undulating smoothly ready to weigh anchor
On the blue horizon, while only the whisper
Of the wind goes by in concise accords.

And those accords the wind carries
Far across the unknown sea.
I dream. Life is sad and I am alone

O when O when in a fiery morning
Will my soul, free and trembling,
Awaken to the sun, to the eternal sun.

DONNA GENOVESE

Tu mi portasti un po' d'alga marina
Nei tuoi capelli, ed un odor di vento,
Che è corso di lontano e giunge grave
D'ardore, era nel tuo corpo bronzino:
— Oh la divina
Semplicità delle tue forme snelle—
Non amore non spasimo, un fantasma,
Un'ombra della necessità che vaga
Serena e ineluttabile per l'anima
E la discioglie in gioia, in incanto serena
Perché per l'infinito lo scirocco
Se la possa portare.
Come è piccolo il mondo e leggero nelle tue mani!

WOMAN FROM GENOA

You brought me a little seaweed
In your hair and a scent of wind
That came from afar and arrives weighted
With warmth on your bronzed body:
—Oh the divine
Artlessness of your slim figure—
Not love not agony, a ghost,
A shade of necessity that wanders
Serenely and ineluctably into the soul
And dissolves it in joy, in serene enchantment
So that the sirocco may carry it
Into infinity.
How small the world is and light in your hands!

A UNA TROIA DAGLI OCCHI FERRIGNI

Coi tuoi piccoli occhi bestiali
Mi guardi e taci e aspetti e poi ti stringi
E mi riguardi e taci. La tua carne
Goffa e pesante dorme intorpidita
Nei sogni primordiali. Prostituta. . . .
Chi ti chiamò alla vita? D'onde vieni?
Dagli acri porti tirreni,
Dalle fiere cantanti di Toscana
O nelle sabbie ardenti voltolata
Fu la tua madre sotto gli scirocchi?
L'immensità t'impresse lo stupore
Nella faccia ferina di sfinge
L'alito brulicante della vita
Tragicamente come a lionessa
Ti disquassa la tua criniera nera
E tu guardi il sacrilego angelo biondo
Che non t'ama e non ami e che soffre
Di te e che stanco ti bacia.

WHORE WITH IRON-GRAY EYES

With your small brutal eyes
You look at me, say nothing, wait, then draw close,
Look at me again and say nothing. Your dull
And lumpish flesh sleeps benumbed
In primordial dreams. Prostitute. . . .
Who called you to life? Where do you come from?
Arid Tyrrhenian ports,
Resounding Tuscan fairs
Or under siroccos was your mother
Rolled over on the burning sand?
Hugeness impressed stupor upon you
In the feral face of a sphinx
The swarming breath of life
Tragically shakes your black mane
As if you were a she-lion
And you look at the profane blond angel
Who loves you not and you love not and who suffers
Because of you and who, tired, kisses you.

SPECIE DI SERENATA
AGRA E FALSA E MELODRAMMATICA

Sui cerchi concentrici di vite quadrilustri
Pieno di trilli d'angeli corrotti
Sui profili
Dagli occhi pesti e dalle labbra molli
Si libra il melodramma:
Il buffo dalla voce grave e fonda
Dal profilo caprino folgorante
Nell'occhio cavo infernale
Canta una canzon d'amore:
Trilla trilla mora pesta
Presto è l'alba, presto è desta.
Usignuolo della notte
O greca dal nero profilo
O bocca rossa come una ferita
O troia incommensurabile
Ed amo le tue pose schife
O triglia condita al ragù
Di gelsomino biacca e baccalà,
O romana delinquente ferina
E te capra languida greca
Dal profilo come bambagia.
E dall'occhio velato e pecorile!

. . . .

SERENADE:
BITTER FALSE MELODRAMATIC

On the concentric spheres of twenty years of existence
Full of warbling by corrupted angels
Melodrama hovers
Over profiles
Of bruised eyes and soft lips:
The comedian with serious and deep voice
With a goat's profile and a hollow
Infernal eye flashing
Sings a song of love:
Warble warble squashed blackberry
Dawn comes soon, the dawn's awake.
Nightingale of the night
O Greek black profile
O red mouth like a wound
O incommensurable whore
And I love your dirty poses
O red mullet pickled in a ragout
Of white lead jasmine and dried codfish,
O bestial delinquent Roman
And you weary Greek goat
With a profile like soft cotton
And an eye veiled and ovine!

. . . .

Io adoro la gaiezza che fa tremare.
Un trillo del basso mi prende
Per le strade deserte.
Gelide incombono le stelle
Così belle e sole come sui monti nevosi
E va la mascherata grottesca melodrammatica
E va come la vita schernitrice
Nei suoi concerti stonati e che prendono
Una tristezza straziante nelle ultime note stridenti
. . . .

Il basso profondo e infernale è la guida
Le donne seguono con ondeggiamenti molli
Le strade suonano al martellare sordo dei passi
La vertigine della fossa mi guarda in silenzio
Il nulla grottesco enorme scende come un vapore
Molle e scipito lento ondeggiante per l'aria.

I adore gaiety that inspires trembling.
A trill of a basso takes hold of me
On the deserted road.
The icy stars overhang
So beautifully and lonely as on snowy mountains
The grotesque melodramatic masquerade goes on
As life the sneerer goes on
In false harmonies that assume
A heartrending sadness in their final strident notes

. . . .

The infernal basso profundo is the guide
The women follow with soft undulations
The road resounds to the dull hammering of steps
The dizziness of the ditch looks at me in silence
Grotesque enormous nothingness descends like a soft
And insipid vapor slowly hesitating in the air.

ERMAFRODITO

Ermafrodito baciò le sue labbra allo specchio
In un quadro profondo
Nerastro appare rosea, biaccosa la carne di lui sullo sfondo
Di Ermafrodito in spasimi molli affogato
Dal paese della chimera eterno e profondo
Dove perdesi l'anima fantasticando
M'apparve affacciato alla superficie del mondo
Ermafrodito risveglio che inanellò l'acque insaziabile
       di giungere al fondo
Ermafrodito in spasimi molli affogato.
Dal fiume maledetto dove non canta la vita
Ti levi talvolta pur nelle notti lunari ed appari
Alla finestra mia colla madreperlacea luna
E stai come uno spettro vigilando il mio cuore
Che si consuma alla luce funerea lunare
La primavera anche ti è amica talvolta
E passi lontano coi venti odorosi
       pei prati
Brucia il cuore al poeta mentre riguardano i bovi;
Ma sempre sopra al mio letto vigila la bocca stanca e
       convulsa
Il vago pallore del volto e delle tue bionde chiome.

HERMAPHRODITE

Hermaphrodite kissed his lips in the mirror
In a deep blackish painting
His flesh wet white in the background appears rosy
From the eternal and profound country of the chimera
Where the soul is lost daydreaming
Hermaphrodite crushed in soft spasms
Seemed to me appearing over the surface of the world
Hermaphrodite awakening ringed the waters, eager to
      reach the depths
Hermaphrodite crushed in soft spasms.
From the damned river where life does not sing
At times you arise even on moonlit nights and appear
At my window with the nacreous moon
And stay like a specter watching over my heart
Which wastes away in lunar funereal light
Even springtime is sometimes friendly to you
And with the fragrant winds you pass at a distance through
      the fields
The heart burns in the poet while the oxen stare;
But ever above my bed the tired and convulsed mouth
      watches
The charming pallor of your face and your blond hair.

BUENOS AIRES

Il bastimento avanza lentamente
Nel grigio del mattino tra la nebbia
Sull'acqua gialla d'un mare fluviale
Appare la città grigia e velata.
Si entra in un porto strano. Gli emigranti
Impazzano e inferocian accalcandosi
Nell'aspra ebbrezza d'imminente lotta.
Da un gruppo d'italiani ch'è vestito
In un modo ridicolo alla moda
Bonearense si gettano arance
Ai paesani stralunati e urlanti.
Un ragazzo dal porto leggerissimo
Prole di libertà, pronto allo slancio
Li guarda colle mani nella fascia
Variopinta ed accenna ad un saluto.
Ma ringhiano feroci gli italiani.

BUENOS AIRES

In the gray of morning the ship
Proceeds slowly in the fog
On the yellow water of a tidal sea
The city appears gray and veiled.
We enter a strange port. The emigrants
Are frantic and become mad as they press
In the harsh frenzy of imminent struggle.
From a group of Italians dressed ridiculously
In the fashion of Buenos Aires
Some throw oranges
To their wide-eyed screaming countrymen.
A boy quite carefree in bearing,
A child of liberty ready to jump,
Looks at them his hands in a varicolored
Sash and nods a greeting.
But the fierce Italians snarl.

MARRADI

Il vecchio castello che ride sereno sull'alto
La valle canora dove si snoda l'azzurro fiume
Che rotto e muggente a tratti canta
    epopea
E sereno riposa in larghi specchi d'azzurro:
Vita e sogno che in fondo alla mistica valle
Agitate l'anima dei secoli passati:
Ora per voi la speranza
Nell'aria ininterrottamente
Sopra l'ombra del bosco che la annega
Sale in lontano appello
Insaziabilmente
Batte al mio cuor che trema di vertigine

MARRADI

In the clear sky the old castle glistens high above
The resonant valley where the blue river
Broken and roaring unwinds and at intervals sings an
      epopee
And lies serene in widening blue mirrors:
Life and dream at the bottom of the mystic valley
You agitate the soul of past centuries:
Uninterruptedly in the air
Hope now rises for you
Over the shadow of the wood that drowns it
In a far-off invocation
Insatiably
It beats at my heart that trembles in dizziness

LA CREAZIONE

Fuor dal cervello enorme e prodigioso
Iddio gettava in bronzo i suoi pensieri
Le forme formidabili ed eterne
Gettava della vita e il mondo sorse
Gli uomini l'adorarono briachi
Dell'aspro succo della verde vita
Vissero e cadder sotto l'occhio immane
Alla sera del giorno portentoso
Sorse il pensiero nelle razze esauste
I vivi sospirarono, la luna
Baciò il sepolcro e suscitò un'ebbrezza
Finché il pensiero sceso nell'inferno
Ne bevve fiamme tanto portentose
Che di contro alla morte ed agli dei
Sublime gittò il carro del destino

THE CREATION

Out of his enormous and prodigious brain
God hurled his thoughts in bronze
He hurled the formidable and eternal forms
Of life and the world rose
Drunk with the harsh sap of green life
Men adored it
Lived and fell under the immense eye
At evening on that portentous day
Thought rose in the exhausted breeds
The living sighed, the moon
Kissed the sepulcher and aroused a frenzy
Till thought descended to hell
Drank its flames so portentous
That against death and the gods
It hurled the chariot of fate sublimely

LA FORZA

Sorvola in cerchio altissimo le costellazioni
E ridiscende sulla potenza torpida dei mari
Che gravita immane sopra del seno del mondo
Erotta dalle sue correnti sorde
La livida scintilla elettrica
Illumina il portento umano
Che pilota la vita nel suo seno
Bruciano insaziabili le fornaci interne del mondo
Ancora
Il corpo dell'uomo si tende e distende.
Un balocco formidabile di raziocinio umano
Irraggia la sua volontà pei cieli
L'energia doma bramisce immane nel motore
Tremano sulle scranne barocche i monarchi belluini
Si sfiancano troni ed altari cementati di sperma
Purifichiamo le donne sotto del peso dei mari.

STRENGTH

It flies over the constellations in the highest sphere
And comes down again on the sea's numbed force
Which tremendously weighs over the breast of the world
Erupted from its deafened currents
The livid electric spark
Illuminates human wonder
That pilots life in its breast
The insatiable internal furnaces of the world still
Burn
The body of man stretches and grows large.
A dreadful toy of human ratiocination
Irradiates its will across the skies
Subdued energy rumbles frightfully in the motor
The beastly monarchs tremble over their baroque chairs
And thrones and altars cemented with sperm collapse
Let us purify the women under the weight of the seas.

O POESIA POESIA POESIA

O poesia poesia poesia
Sorgi, sorgi, sorgi
Su dalla febbre elettrica del selciato notturno.
Sfrenati dalle elastiche silhouettes equivoche
Guizza nello scatto e nell'urlo improvviso
Sopra l'anonima fucileria monotona
Delle voci instancabili come i flutti
Stride la troia perversa al quadrivio
Poiché l'elegantone le rubò il cagnolino
Saltella una cocotte cavalletta
Da un marciapiede a un altro tutta verde
E scortica le mie midolla il raschio ferrigno del tram
Silenzio—un gesto fulmineo
Ha generato una pioggia di stelle
Da un fianco che piega e rovina sotto il colpo
        prestigioso
In un mantello di sangue vellutato occhieggiante
Silenzio ancora. Commenta secco
E sordo un revolver che annuncia
E chiude un altro destino

THE VIOLENT SOUNDS OF NIGHT

O poetry poetry poetry
Rise rise rise up
From the electric fever of the pavement at night.
Released from elastic indistinct silhouettes
It flashes in an outburst and in a sudden shriek
Over the anonymous unvarying fusilade
Of voices untiring as waves
At the crossroads a depraved whore screams
Because a fop stole her puppy
A cocotte skips about as a grasshopper
From one sidewalk to another entirely green
The screeching iron of the trolley tears at my marrow
Silence — a sudden gesture
Has generated a shower of stars
From a flank that folds up and crashes down under a
        brilliant stroke
In a mantle of ogling velvety blood
Silence again. Abrupt and hollow
A revolver speaks that announces
And concludes another fatality

O L'ANIMA VIVENTE DELLE COSE

O l'anima vivente delle cose
O poesia deh baciala deh chiudila come il sole di Maggio
Non vana come i sogni dei mattini
Torpido. Scintilli il tuo pensiero
Sulle forme molteplici
Che muovono cantano e stridono
Eletrizzate nel sole
Anima oscura del mondo
Son le tue forme molteplici
Che tratte dal sonno alla vita
Ora avviluppano il mondo
Io confitto nel masso
Ti guardo o dea forza
Tu mi sferzi e mi sciogli e mi lanci
Nel tuo fremente torbido mare
O poesia siimi tu faro
Siimi tu faro e porterò un voto laggiù
Sotto degli infrenati archi marini
Dell'alterna tua chiesa azzurra e bianca
Là dove aurora fiammea s'affranca
Da un arco eburneo, a magici confini
Genova Genova Genova

I, NAILED TO A BOULDER

O poetry for pity's sake kiss the living soul of things
And shut it in like the May sun
Not vain as the dreams of sluggish
Mornings. May your thought sparkle
On multiple forms
That move sing scream
Electrified in the sun
Obscure soul of the world
Your multiple forms exist
That drawn from sleep to life
Now entangle the world
I nailed to a boulder
Look at you O goddess strength
You scourge melt hurl me
Into your trembling turbid sea
O poetry be to me a beacon
Be to me a beacon and I will carry an oblation down there
Under the unchecked arches of the sea
Of your church alternately blue and white
There where the flaming aurora frees itself
From an ivory arc toward magical frontiers
Genoa Genoa Genoa

O POESIA TU PIÙ NON TORNERAI

O poesia tu più non tornerai
Eleganza eleganza
Arco teso della bellezza.
La carne è stanca, s'annebbia il cervello, si stanca
Palme grigie senza odore si allungano
Davanti al deserto del mare
Non campane, fischi che lacerano l'azzurro
Non canti, grida
E su questa aridità furente
La forma leggera dai sacri occhi bruni
Ondulante portando il tabernacolo del seno:
I cubi degli alti palazzi torreggiano
Minacciando enormi sull'erta ripida
Nell'ardore catastrofico

THIS RAGING ARIDITY

O poetry you will no longer return
Elegance elegance
Taut arc of beauty
The flesh is tired, the brain grows dim, becomes tired
Gray odorless palms stretch out
Before the desert of the sea
No bells, whistles to tear the sky apart,
No songs, screams
And on this raging aridity
A light figure with sacred brown eyes
Carrying undulating the tabernacle of her breast:
The cubes of the tall enormous palaces
Towering and threatening on the precipitous slope
In catastrophic ardor

NELLA PAMPA GIALLASTRA
IL TRENO ARDENTE

Nella pampa giallastra il treno ardente
Correva sempre in corsa vittoriosa
E travolto vertiginosamente
Il vergine infinito, senza posa

Mi baciava sul viso, e il continente
Grottesco e enorme cambiava la posa — immantinente,
     senza posa
Così il mio libro: ed ecco che:

Ecco che viene colle gambe storte
Il mio sonetto a voi per salutare
Accettatelo bene per le rare
Virtù che porta nelle rime attorte.
E quando venga l'ora della morte
Ritorni la vostr'anima a brucare
A voi che cose peregrine e rare
Accarezzaste nelle gambe storte

.   .   .   .

Io cerco una parola
Una sola parola per:
Sputarvi in viso, sfondarvi, [. . . . . . .]
Merda — per ora
Al chimico che scoprirà di meglio

THE FIERY TRAIN
ON THE TAWNY PAMPAS

The fiery train on the tawny pampas
Always ran its triumphant race
And vertiginously upset
The virginal infinite endlessly

Kissed me on the face and the grotesque and enormous
Continent changed its posture—immediately
    endlessly
So my book: and here it:

Here it comes on crippled feet
My sonnet a salute to you
Accept it kindly, its rare virtue
To bear distorted rhymes off-beat.
And when the hour of death is meet
O may your soul return to you
To graze as you caress a few
Odd things between your crippled feet

.   .   .   .

I look for a word
A unique word for:
Spit in your face, ram through you, [. . . . . . .]
Shit—for now
To the chemist who will discover better than this

129

Sia dato il premio Nobel:
Una parola — dinamite fetida
Che immelmi lo scarlatto del vostro sangue porcino
E vi stritoli la spina dorsale
E moriate nel viscidume vomitorio melmoso delle
        vostre midolla

May he be given the Nobel prize:
A word—stinking dynamite
That may dirty the scarlet of your porcine blood
And crush your dorsal spine
So may you die in the slimy mossy vomit of
        your pulp

UOMO, SIN DAI PRIMEVI TORBIDI

Uomo, sin dai primevi torbidi
La tua maschia figura
Sul fondo azzurro del mar tremolante
S'oscura.
Ma non oggi la morte attorno sui campi
Il vitale frastuono
Te cinge potenza raccolta e pensosa
L'antico tuo trono
In lunghe ombre lambe forza
O pastore del gregge infinito
Del mondo fenomenale.
La donna sotto gli archi a riguardare
È buono, della città fremente,
Sogni composti dell'onde plurifeconde sue,
Sfinge silenziosa ridente elastica
Trascivolante su rabescati colori
Ma te uomo sullo stridore violento
In mezzo alla via scabra
Dove bramisce e geme serpentina la forza
Al palpito alato del sole e del vento
Per l'antica e feconda voluttà,
Nell'antica e feconda volontà
A te congemini.

MAN: FECUND LUST AND WILL

O man from your turbulent beginnings
Your virile figure
Over the blue depth of the trembling sea
Is darkened.
But not today death about the fields
The vital hubbub
Embraces you with its gathered and grave power
Strength in long shadows
Skims your ancient throne
O shepherd of the endless flock
Of the phenomenal world.
It is good to look at a woman
Under the arches of the trembling city
Dreams made of her overly ripened waves
Sphinx silent laughing buoyant
Gliding through on colored arabesques
But you man above the violent stridency
In the middie of the rough road
Where serpentine strength roars and moans
To the swift throb of sun and wind
For the ancient and fecund lust
In the ancient and fecund will
Both geminate in you.

PEI VICHI FONDI TRA IL PALPITO ROSSO

Pei vichi fondi tra il palpito rosso
Dei fanali, sull'ombra illanguidita:
Al vento di preludio di un gran mare
Ricchissimo accampato in fondo all'ombra
Che mi cullava di venture incerte
Io me n'andavo nella sera ambigua
Nell'alito salso umano
Tra nimbi screziati sfuggenti
In alto da ogive orientali
Col caro mare nel petto
Col caro mare nell'anima
Or tremo. L'apparizione fu ineffabile
Una grazia lombarda in alto sale
Ventoso dolce e querula salìa
(Vicendavano infaticabilmente
Nuvole e stelle nel cielo serale)
L'accompagnava un vecchio combattente
Ischeletrito da sorte nemica
Dallo sguardo diritto, umile ed alto:
Gioventù, gioventù ravvolta in veli
Luminosi, tradita dalla sorte
Giovinetta trafitta che invermiglia
Il sangue sulle labbra orribilmente
O stretta al magro padre sola figlia.
Di sotto il manto rosso del fanale

TREMBLING OF TOMBS

Through the deep alleys among the red throbbing
Of street lamps in the flagging shadow:
Facing the wind foretelling a heavy sea
Most richly encamped in the depth of shadow
That lulled me to uncertain adventure
I went off into the ambiguous evening
In the salty human exhalation
Among the speckled aureoles escaping
Up high from the oriental ogives
With the dear sea in my breast
With the dear sea in my soul
Now I tremble. The apparition was ineffable
A girl from Lombardy sweet and querulous
Rose in the windy salty height
(Clouds and stars in the evening sky
Alternated tirelessly)
Humble and sublime, his glance direct,
Reduced to a skeleton by adversity
An old fighter accompanied her:
Youth, youth wrapped up
In luminous veils, betrayed by life,
Young girl transfixed whose lips
Her blood reddens shockingly
O only daughter clasped to a shrunken father.
Under the red mantle of the street lamp

Io l'attesi e la vidi che sul labbro
Sul labbro del suo viso macilente
Le risplendeva un carminio spettrale

O vita sarcastica atroce
O miseria nefanda intravista
All'angolo di un vico lubrico nella sera ambigua
Al palpitare inquieto dei fanali
Animatrice delle vampe fantastiche
Di luce ed ombra vanenti col vento,
Di rumori cupi e di silenzii in risacca
Pei vichi stretti è vivo solo il rosso
Dei fanali, le stelle s'avvicendan
Colle nubi ed il vecchio si consiglia
Per salire alla piazza in alto ardente
Di luci e lampi, a lui stretta la figlia
Nel silenzio caldissimo ambiguo
Della notte voluttuosa
Scuotevasi il mare profondo:
Era caldo il silenzio sullo sfondo
Le navi inermi, drizzate in balzi
Terrifici al cielo
Allucinate in aurora
Elettrica inumana risplendente
Alla prora per l'occhio incandescente.
Un passo solitario,
Un'ombra di un'ombra sui quais.
La città stava sepolta

I waited for her and on her lips
On the lips of her emaciated face
A spectral vermilion glittered

O sarcastic atrocious life
O abominable glimpse of misery
At the corner of an indecent alley in the ambiguous evening
To the unquiet throbbing of street lamps
The creative spirit of the fantastic blaze
Of light and shade vanished with the wind
Of gloomy noises and silences in the backwash
Through the narrow alleys only the red
Of the street lamps is alive, the stars
And clouds alternate, and the old man resolves
To climb high up to the piazza burning
With lights and flashes, his daughter clasped to him
In the warmest ambiguous silence
Of the voluptuous night
The deep sea shook itself:
Silence was hot in the background
The defenseless ships rising
In terrific leaps to the sky
Dazzled by the untamed
Electric aurora resplendent
At the prow through the incandescent eye.
A solitary step
A shadow of a shadow on the docks:
The city lay buried

Nella luce uniforme fiammeggiante
E le navi angosciate
Mi suadevano all'ultima avventura
Nella notte di Giugno
Vasta terribile e pura
Ritorno inesorabilmente a te
Riscossa dal tuo sogno
Acqua di mare amaro
Che esali nella notte:
Verso le eterne rotte
Il mio destino prepara
Mare che batti come un cuore stanco
Violentato dalla voglia atroce
Di un Essere insaziato che si strugge
Della sua forza terrifica ardente:
Nave che soffri e vegli
Coll'occhio disumano
E al destino lontano
Sempre sopra del vano
Ondeggiare tu pensi
E m'arde e m'arde il cuore
Nella notte serena
Che tutta è per voi piena
Di fremiti di tombe.

In flaming uniform light
And the anguished ships
Persuaded me to final adventure
On a June night
Vast terrible and pure
I return inexorably to you
Rescued from your dream
Water of a bitter sea
That you exhale in the night:
O sea prepare my destiny
Toward eternal routes
As you beat like a tired heart
Forced by the atrocious will
Of an insatiable Being that destroys itself
By its terrible blazing strength:
O ship as you suffer and watch
With an inhuman eye
And you think of a destiny far-off
Ever above the vain
Undulation
And my heart burns and burns
In the starlit night
Totally filled for you
With the trembling of tombs.

SPIAGGIA, SPIAGGIA

Spiaggia, spiaggia.
Giunse il battello e riposa
Nel crepuscolo e l'anima divina
Costella di elettriche lune
Gli alberi
Il paesaggio è mitico
Di navi all'infinito:
Dal battello capace
Ascendono i tesori della sera
Calida di felicità:
Ininterrottamente.
Triangoli magici
Di lampade elettriche
S'incastonan nel crepuscolo
I viaggiatori oziano sul molo
I bambini rincorronsi sul molo
Son giunti al porto di felicità.
Il battello si scarica
Ininterrottamente
Instancabilmente
Ha finito il suo compito e s'accende
Delle luci d'argento
La bandiera è calata
Il mare e il cielo è d'oro
Splende sugli alberi felicità

IN THE THUNDERING TWILIGHT

Seashore, seashore.
The ship arrived and lies
In the twilight and a divine spirit
Spangles the masts
With electric moons
The landscape is mythical
With ships toward infinity:
From a capacious vessel
The treasures of the evening
Balmy in happiness rise:
Uninterruptedly.
Magic triangles
Of electric lamps
Are mounted in the twilight
The travelers lounge on the breakwater
The children chase each other on the breakwater
They have reached the port of happiness.
The vessel unloads
Uninterruptedly
Untiringly
Has finished its job and kindles
Silver lights
The flag is lowered
The sea and the sky are golden
Happiness glistens on the masts

A frotte s'avventurano
I viaggiatori alla città sonante
Che stende le sue piazze e le sue vie
La poesia mediterranea
S'arronda in pietra di cenere
S'ingolfa pei vichi antichi e profondi.
Fragore di vita
Gioia intensa e fugace
Velario d'oro di felicità
È il cielo ove il sole ricchissimo
Lasciò le sue spoglie preziose,
E la città comprende
E s'accende
E la fiamma titilla ed assorbe
I resti magnificenti del sole
E intesse un sudario d'oblio
Divino per gli uomini stanchi.
Perdute nel crepuscolo tonante
Ombre di viaggiatori
Vanno per la Superba
Terribili e grotteschi come i ciechi

In groups the travelers venture
Into the city, its clamor
Reaching into the squares and streets
Mediterranean poetry
Makes the rounds of ashen stone
Is engulfed by the ancient deep alleys.
Roar of life
Intense and fugitive joy
Curtain of golden happiness
The sky is where the richest sun
Left its precious spoil
And the city understands
And lights up
And the flame titillates and swallows up
The magnificent residues of the sun
And interweaves a shroud of oblivion
Divine for tired men.
Lost in the thundering twilight
Shadows of travelers
Walk through La Superba
Fearful and grotesque as the blind

DALL'ALTO GIÙ PER LA CHINA RIPIDA

Dall'alto giù per la china ripida
O corridore tu voli in ritmo
Infaticabile. Bronzeo il tuo corpo dal turbine
Tu vieni nocchiero del cuore insaziato.
Sotto la rupe alpestre tra grida di turbe rideste
Alla vita primeva, gagliarda d'ebbrezze.
Bronzeo il tuo corpo dal turbine
Discende con lancio leggero
Vertiginoso silenzio. Rocciosa catastrofe ardente d'intorno
E fosti serpente anelante col ritmo concorde del palpito
    indomo
Fuggisti nell'onda di grido fremente, col cuore dei mille
    con te.
Come di fiera in caccia di dietro ti vola una turba.

RUNNER IN FLIGHT

From a height downward on a steep slope
You fly, O runner, in untiring
Rhythm. Your body bronzed by the whirlwind
You arrive leader of the unsated heart.
Under the Alpine cliff among cries of crowds awakened to
Primeval life, bold with rapture
Your body bronzed by the whirlwind
Descends with a light leap
In dizzy silence. A stony catastrophe burning on every side
You were a snake gasping in a steady rhythm of untamed
        throbbing
You fled in a wave of trembling cries, the hearts of
        thousands with you.
As in chasing a wild beast a crowd flies behind you.

SORGA LA LARVA DI ANTICO SOGNO

Sorga la larva di antico sogno
Dai confini del nulla ed a quel sogno
Tutto il mio tardo cuore è incatenato.
Sventoli, contro il vento
Battagli: i cigli lunghi
Traenti in arco tendi
Sotto il morione nero
Che una penna commenta. . . .
Ridente in grazia ovale
Più fine del velluto
Incedi ingenua ardita
Agile come vela
Nel vento sui sassi di Prè.
Nel vento che ti ha presa
I lunghi passi accelera:
Nel vento di scirocco
In strana serenata
Udrai forse novella
Questa notte dal mare:
Supina sul tuo letto
Pensare nel languore
Catastrofi lontane
Mentre colle sue antenne
E le sue luci un grande
Cimitero il tuo porto

146

ENORMOUS TOMB OF THE SEA

May the ghost of an old dream rise
From the limits of nothingness and to that dream
All my sluggish heart is shackled.
You flap; against the wind
You struggle: you stretch
Your long eyebrows in an arc
Drawn under the black helmet
That a feather annotates. . . .
Smiling in oval grace
Finer than velvet
You strut naturally impertinent
Light as a sail
In the wind on the stones of Prè
In the wind that has seized you
That speeds up your long steps:
In the wind of the sirocco
In a strange serenade
Perhaps you will hear news
This night from the sea:
Supine on your bed
To think in weariness
Of distant catastrophes
While with its antennae
And its lights your port seems to you
A great cemetery

Ti sembri e ti spaventi
Il naufragio e l'amore.

. . . .

Ne la notte voluttuosa
Scuotevasi il mare profondo
Caldo ambiguo il silenzio sullo sfondo
Le navi inermi drizzavansi in balzi
Terrifici al cielo
Allucinate di aurora
Elettrica inumana, risplendente
A la poppa ne l'occhio incandescente.
Un passo solitario
Un'ombra di un'ombra sui quais:
La città giace sepolta
Ne la luce uniforme fiammeggiante
E le navi angosciate
Mi suadono all'ultima avventura
Ne la notte di Giugno
Vasta terribile e pura. . . .
Acqua di mare amaro
Che esali ne la notte
Verso le eterne rotte
Il mio destin prepara:
Mare che batti come un cuore stanco
Violentato da la voglia atroce
Dell'Essere insaziato che s'inquieta
E si quieta ne la forza sola. . . .
Mi sperda con te o nave,

That frightens you
As a shipwreck or love.

.   .   .   .

In the voluptuous night
The deep sea shook itself
Warm and ambiguous the silence in the background
The defenseless ships rising
In terrific leaps to the sky
Dazzled by the untamed
Electric aurora, resplendent
At the prow in the incandescent eye.
A solitary step
A shadow of a shadow on the docks:
The city lies buried
In flaming uniform light
And the anguished ships
Persuade me to final adventure
On a June night
Vast terrible and pure. . . .
Water of a bitter sea
That you exhale in the night
Prepare my destiny
Toward eternal routes:
Sea as you beat like a tired heart
Forced by the atrocious will
Of an unsatiable Being that is restless
And rests on its strength alone. . . .
May I vanish with you, O ship,

Nave che soffri e vegli
Coll'occhio disumano
E al destino lontano
Sempre sopra del vano
Ondeggiare tu pensi. . . .
Così chiusi il mio patto
Ne la notte serena
Su l'inquieta piena
Tomba enorme del mare.

O ship as you suffer and watch
With an inhuman eye
And to a destiny far-off
Ever above the vain
Undulation you think. . . .
So I closed my pact
In the starlit night
On the uneasy full
Enormous tomb of the sea.

QUATTRO LIRICHE
PER SIBILLA ALERAMO

I PILONI FANNO IL FIUME PIÙ BELLO

I piloni fanno il fiume più bello
E gli archi fanno il cielo più bello
Negli archi la tua figura.
Più pura nell'azzurro è la luce d'argento
Più bella la tua figura.
Più bella la luce d'argento nell'ombra degli archi
Più bella della bionda Cerere la tua figura.

SUL PIÙ ILLUSTRE PAESAGGIO

Sul più illustre paesaggio
Ha passeggiato il ricordo
Col vostro passo di pantera
Sul più illustre paesaggio
Il vostro passo di velluto
E il vostro sguardo di vergine violata
Il vostro passo silenzioso come il ricordo
Affacciata al parapetto
Sull'acqua corrente
I vostri occhi forti di luce.

FOUR LYRICS
FOR SIBILLA ALERAMO

BLONDE CERES

The pylons make the river more beautiful
And the arches the sky more beautiful
In the arches your figure.
More pure is the light of silver in the sky
More beautiful your figure
More beautiful the light of silver in the shadow of the arches
Your figure more beautiful than blonde Ceres.

YOU IN REMEMBRANCE

On the most famous landscape
Remembrance has strolled
With your panther-like step
On the most famous landscape
Your velvet step
Your glance of a violated virgin
Your step silent as remembrance
Looking out over the parapet
Above running water
Your eyes large with light.

IN UN MOMENTO

In un momento
Sono sfiorite le rose
I petali caduti
Perché io non potevo dimenticare le rose
Le cercavamo insieme
Abbiamo trovato delle rose
Erano le sue rose erano le mie rose
Questo viaggio chiamavamo amore
Col nostro sangue e colle nostre lagrime facevamo le rose
Che brillavano un momento al sole del mattino
Le abbiamo sfiorite sotto il sole tra i rovi
Le rose che non erano le nostre rose
Le mie rose le sue rose

P.S. E così dimenticammo le rose.

VI AMAI NELLA CITTA DOVE PER SOLE

Vi amai nella città dove per sole
Strade si posa il passo illanguidito
Dove una pace tenera che piove
A sera il cuor non sazio e non pentito
Volge a un'ambigua primavera in viole
Lontane sopra il cielo impallidito.

JOURNEY WE CALLED LOVE

In a moment
Roses are faded
The petals fallen
Since I could not forget roses
We looked for them together
We found some roses
They were her roses they were my roses
This journey we called love
With our blood and tears we made roses
That sparkled a moment in the morning sun
Under the sun in the thornbush
We made the roses fade that were not our roses
My roses her roses

P.S. And so we forgot the roses.

LOVE: A SPRINGTIME EVENING

I loved you in the city where
The weakened footstep rests on lonely streets
Where a tender peace diffused at evening
Turns the unsated and unrepentant heart
Toward an ambiguous springtime in
Violet distances over a sky turned pale.

CANTO PROLETARIO ITALO-FRANCESE

Come delle torri d'acciaio
Nel cuore bruno della sera
Il mio spirito ricrea
Per un bacio taciturno
Là se c'è un fulvo giardino
E se è elegiaca con il turchino
Sull'Alpe c'è una scaglia di lavoro
Del povero italiano? non si sa
Tra i pioppi
Al margine degli occhi
Bruni della sera
Se c'è una pastorella non si sa
Perché fan vano le torri
Al taglio di un pioppo che brilla
Come delle torri d'acciaio
Nel cuor bruno della sera
Il mio spirito ricrea
Per un bacio taciturno
Italia
Ti amo con smisurato dolore
E brilla la scaglia del cuore
Del tuo lavoro che si tingerà
Sotto la luce dei picchi irsuti
Hai fatto strada per le montagne
Con poco canto con molto vino

FRANCO-ITALIAN PROLETARIAN SONG

As steel towers
In the dark heart of evening
My spirit becomes new
By a taciturn kiss
If there there is a reddish garden
And if an elegiac deep blue lies
Over the Alps is there a smitch of work
By the poor Italian? No one knows
Among the poplars
At the edge of the dark
Eyes of evening
If there is a shepherdess no one knows
Since the towers stand useless
Near the profile of a poplar that shines
As steel towers
In the dark heart of evening
My spirit becomes new
By a taciturn kiss
Italy
I love you with immeasurable aching
And a chip of the heart shines
In your work that will be dyed
Under the light of bristling peaks
You have built a road through the mountains
With little song and much wine

Sei arrivata vicino
Fin dove si poteva arrivar
Senza interrogare la giubba rossa delle stelle
Hai sfondato finche si poteva arrivare
Fin che sei andata a riposare
Laggiù nello straniero suol
Italia non ti posso lasciare
La scaglia dell'italiano senza cuore
Brilla: stai fida: l'onore
Te lo venderemo con una nuova verginità.

L'edera gira le torri
È la vigna della tua passione
Italia che fai processione
Con il badile prendi il fucile ti tocca andar
Fora la giubba rossa delle stelle
Questa volta con il cannone
Italia che fai processione
Con il badile prendi il fucile
Guarda il nemico ti tocca andar
Guarda il nemico che poi non t'importa
Ti sei fatta a forzare la pietra
Prendi coraggio se batti la porta
Questa volta ti si aprirà
Cara Italia che t'importa
Ti sei fatta a forzare la pietra
Prendi il coraggio questa volta
Che la porta si aprirà.

You went as far
As you could go
Without questioning the red jacket of the stars
You broke through as far as you could go
Until you went to sleep
Down there on alien soil
Italy I cannot leave you
Of the heartless Italian a chip
Shines: Rest assured: we will sell your
Honor with a new maidenhead.

The ivy winds around the towers
It is the vineyard of your passion
Italy as you parade
Take the gun with the shovel you have to go
Pierce the red jacket of the stars
This time with cannon
Italy as you parade
Take the gun with the shovel
Look at the enemy you have to go
Look at the enemy for then you do not care
You are compelled to force stone
Take courage if you knock at the door
This time it will open to you
Dear Italy what does it matter to you
You are compelled to force stone
Take courage this time
For the door will open to you.

Nel paesaggio lente si spostavano le rondinelle. Il paesaggio era costituito dal ponte oltre il secondo fiume. Como nel paessagio l'oro e l'azzurro dei tramonti decrepiti si fosse cambiato in verde vedevo torri. . . .

Come delle torri d'acciaio
Nel cuore bruno della sera
Il mio spirito ricrea
Per un bacio taciturno.

The swallows traveled slowly over the landscape. The landscape was made by the bridge beyond the second river. As over the landscape the gold and blue of decrepit sunsets had changed to green I saw towers. . . .

As steel towers
In the dark heart of evening
My spirit becomes new
By a taciturn kiss.

BIOLOGIA

Essendo una carogna in decomposizione abbraccio l'universo. Guardate il mio cromatismo, i miei verdi e violetti. Guardate al resto, il mio scheletro, ci sono dunque esisto.

P.S. A volte infilo una camicia rossa per spaventare i passeri.

Monsieur Pappin, per la mia ingenuità naturale volli fare lo sbirro ma poi vidi la filosofia.

BIOLOGY

Since I am carrion in decomposition I embrace the universe. Look at my chromatism, my greens and violets. Look at the rest, my skeleton. Here I am so I exist.

P.S. At times I put on a red shirt to scare the sparrows.

Monsieur Pappin, because of my natural innocence I wanted to be a cop but then I saw philosophy.

PROSPECTUS III

Sulla panca dell'ospedale trovo: Cara mamma. L'artista ingenuo ha fatto accanto sulla panca il ritratto ingenuo della sua mamma stecchita abbandonata un occhio su e l'altro giù. Accanto sulla panca incominicia nella lettera un mistero che non sa spiegare:

"Cara mamma

"Nella chiesa del mio paese gli arcipreti cantano con voce di bue. L'Italia siede nel porto d'Ostia sotto l'arco d'oltremare volta al limo del Tevere la faccia, ed eternamente giovane tra ortaggi mitologici passeggia col suo passo di belva niciana. A mezzogiorno nel vecchio chiostro a lunette imbiancate con affreschi di santi insulsi la voce dei caporali rintrona terribilmente. Al rombo del cannon. Il treno coi vagoni decorati di frasche sportive arriva. I vagoni rossi coi nostri soldati. Dentro una persona gentile, certo una donna, ha messo dei mazzi di gigli che riempiono d'odore tutto il vagone. Il treno parte, cantano, la Falterona gira, sul solco, l'odore del giglio. Il treno batte con dei preaccordi di chitarra, per scatatura abrupta dei colli un grido di tre note lungamente canta."

PROSPECTUS III

On the bench in the hospital I find: Dear mama. The ingenuous artist has drawn nearby on the bench the ingenuous portrait of his dried-up forsaken mother one eye up the other down. Nearby on the bench there is in his letter an enigma he knows not how to explain:

"Dear mama

"In the church in my village the archpriests sing with the voices of oxen. Italy lies at Ostia's port under the arc overseas, her face turned to the mud of the Tiber, and eternally young she walks with the tread of a Nietzschean beast among mythological vegetables. At noon in the old cloister with whitewashed lunettes and frescoes of insipid saints the speech of corporals resounds terribly. To the rumble of cannon. The train with cars decorated with sportive foliage arrives. The red cars with our soldiers. Inside, a kind person, certainly a woman, has arranged bunches of lilies that fill the whole car with fragrance. The train leaves, they sing, the Falterona turns, toward the furrow, the fragrances of lily. The train pulsates to the chords of a guitar, up the abrupt climb of the hills a trisyllabic yell is chanted for a time."

4

Alcuni credono di dare il senso della loro profondità coll'estensione del loro lazzaronismo.

7

L'arte è espressione. Ciò farebbe supporre una realtà. L'Italia è come fu sempre: teologica.

8

Quando un solo italiano, ragazzo s'intende, penserà a sputare sulla tomba di Machiavelli?

9

Viene alle lettere una generazione di ladruncoli. Chi vi insegnò l'arte del facil vivere fanciulli?

10

Il popolo d'Italia non canta più. Non vi sembra questa la più grande sciagura nazionale?

11

Oh *parvenu!* tu sei la rovina.

12

Teatro futurista. Scena rovesciata. C'è un morto sulla scena. Si alza, riceve una coltellata, letica, gioca, abbraccia. Questo ci ha fatto pensare ai casi nostri. Si affermava tra i

4

Some believe they give the sense of their profundity by the extension of their rascality.

7

Art is expression. This should imply a reality. Italy is as it ever was: theological.

8

When will even one Italian, a boy to be sure, think of spitting on Machiavelli's tomb?

9

A generation of petty thieves came to literature. Who taught you the art of easy life, children?

10

The people of Italy no longer sing. Doesn't this seem to you the greatest national calamity?

11

Oh *parvenu!* You are our ruination.

12

Futurist theater. Topsy-turvy scene. There is a dead body on the stage. It rises, is stabbed, fights, plays, embraces. This has made us think of our actions. The geniality of the scenic

futuristi la genialità dell'idea scenica. Purtroppo il pubblico è più spiritoso dell'autore.

13

Sembra veramente che il tempo dei filosofi sia finito e cominci l'epoca dei poeti, l'età dell'oro scongiurata così ostinatamente dai filosofi economisti. Nel teatro di cui sopra i poeti hanno il diritto di morir di fame sulla scena, di fronte al critico neutralista e *boche*. Il pubblico tace e quasi acconsente.

15

Non dare all'uomo nulla: ma togli a lui qualche cosa e aiutalo a portarla. Dopo avermi squadrato, voltato e rivoltato e fatto i conti in tasca il benevolo poliziotto mi lasciò andare accompagnandomi con un lungo sguardo che mi parve di protezione. È certo almeno che per un po' mi sentìi più leggero. Questo mi succede leggendo un libro: anche leggendo un libro.

16

Infine confesso: Non amo i meridionali. Questa è stata una delle cause della mia rovina. Non amo gli scolari dei meridionali. Questo mi ha messo in una situazione intollerabile. Passo passo arrivai al pangermanesimo e alla logica di Louvain. Cherchez . . . *la femme? Non, cherchez la vache*. La causa della guerra europea sono le donne, *come elles ont été*, i peggiori *parvenu*. (Perché una donna mi disse pitocco quando ero già coperto di sputi?)

idea was affirming itself among the futurists. Unfortunately the public is more witty than the author.

13

It truly seems that the time of philosophers is ended and the epoch of poets, the golden age so obstinately exorcised by the philosopher-economists, begun. In the theater cited above, poets have the right to starve on the stage before the neutralist critic and *boche*. The public is silent and almost acquiesces.

15

Give man nothing: but take away something from him and help him carry it. After having sized me up, turned me around and around, scrutinized my wealth, the benevolent policeman let me go, following me with a long seemingly protective look. It is certain that at least for a little while I felt somewhat relieved. This happens to me reading a book: even reading a book.

16

Finally I admit: I dislike southerners. This has been one of the reasons for my ruin. I do not like these students of the southerners. This has placed me in an intolerable situation. Little by little I arrived at Pan-Germanism and at the logic of Louvain. *Cherchez . . . la femme? Non, cherchez la vache.* Women are the cause of the European war, *comme elles on été,* the worst *parvenu.* (Why did a woman call me a beggar when I was already covered with spit?)

17

A diciott'anni rinchiusa la porta della prigione piangendo gridai: Governo ideale che hai messo alla porta ma tanta ma tanta canaglia morale.

18

Mi sono sempre battuto in condizioni così sfavorevoli che desidererei farlo alla pari. Sono molto modesto e non vi domando, amici, altro segno che il gesto. Il resto non vi riguarda.

17

At eighteen, after the door of the prison was shut, I screamed weeping, O ideal government, you ejected so much, so much moral scum.

18

I always fought under such unfavorable conditions that I should like to do it on even terms. I am quite modest and I do not ask you, friends, for any other sign than a gesture. The rest does not concern you.

2

Nel giro del ritorno eterno vertiginoso l'immagine muore immediatamente.

3

L'azzurro è il colore della dissoluzione, le ali assomigliano a *quelque chose de bleu*.

Il *bleu* del cielo fiorentino, *l'azur mystique de Baudelaire ce n'est pas ça.*

OBSERVATIONS: II

2

In the cycle of eternal dizzy return the image dies instantly.

3

Blue is the color of disintegration, the wings resemble *quelque chose de bleu.*

The *bleu* of the Florentine sky, *l'azur mystique de Baudelaire ce n'est pas ça.*

IL SECONDO STADIO DELLO SPIRITO. . .

Il secondo stadio dello spirito è lo stadio mediterraneo. Deriva direttamente dal naturalismo. La vita quale è la conosciamo: ora facciamo il sogno della vita in blocco. Anche il misticismo è uno stadio ulteriore della vita in blocco, ma è una forma dello spirito sempre speculativa, sempre razionale, sempre inibitoria in cui il mondo è volontà e rappresentazione: ancora, volontà e rappresentazione che del mondo fa la base di un cono luminoso i cui raggi si concentrano in un punto dell'infinito, nel Nulla, in Dio. Sì: scorrere sopra la vita questo sarebbe necessario questa è l'unica arte possibile. Primo fra tutti i musici sarebbe colui il quale non conoscesse che la tristezza della felicità più profonda e nessun'altra tristezza: una tale musica non è mai esistita ancora. Nietzsche è un Wagner del pensiero. La susseguenza dei suoi pensieri è assolutamente barbara, uguale alla musica wagneriana. In ciò unicamente nell'originalità barbaramente balzante e irrompente dei suoi pensieri sta la sua forza di sovvertimento e tutto anela alla distruzione tanto in Wagner come in lui.

THE SECOND PHASE OF THE SPIRIT

The second phase of the spirit is Mediterranean. It derives directly from naturalism. We know life as it is: now we have the dream of life as a whole. Mysticism also is an ulterior phase of life as a whole, but it is a form of the spirit ever speculative, ever rational, ever restrictive, in which the world is will and representation: again, will and representation which make of the world the base of a luminous cone whose rays concentrate in a point of the infinite, in Nothingness, in God. Yes: to skim over life this would be necessary, this is the only possible art. First among all the musicians would be he who knew only sadness of the deepest happiness and no other sadness; again, such a music has never existed. Nietzsche is a Wagner of thought. The succession of his thoughts is absolutely barbaric, equal to Wagnerian music. In this uniquely, in the barbarically bouncing and breaking originality of his thoughts, is his strength of subversion, and everything yearns for destruction in Wagner as well as in him.

TRANSLATOR'S NOTE

This selection of Campana's poetry is taken from *Orphic Songs*, which the poet saw through the press, and from work that came to light after his death. Ten years later in 1942, Enrico Falqui, an indefatigable editor, entitled a number of poems by their first lines. Without doing violence to Campana's poetry, I have made viable substitutions from the poems themselves. With the facing Italian text before him, the purist may still prefer "Through the Deep Alleys among the Red Throbbing" to "Trembling of Tombs," but I submit that this and other titles ("This Raging Aridity," "The Violent Sounds of Night") are also in keeping with the elemental fury that is so great a part of Campana's poetry.

As for Campana's capricious punctuation, I have introduced an occasional comma, a parenthesis, or a dash to clarify ambiguities.

I have stayed close to the text without being slavish. Where Italian metrics, tonality, accent, etc. did not accommodate themselves to English speech, I followed the cadence of the sentence. Sometimes a word in the Italian (e.g., *ondulava*) had its identical counterpart (undulated) in the English, yet its surface meaning did not resolve the image in "Three Florentine Girls Walk":

> Ondulava sul passo verginale
> Ondulava la chioma musicale

Since the little girls were walking abreast, I took liberties with the literal "virginal step" and introduced a comma in the second line after the verb to avoid an image of decapitation:

> Rolled with a virginal gait
> Rolled, head of hair like music

and I concluded the poem by translating *marcia militare* into French; the phrase is common to our speech:

> E sei piedini in marcia militare
> And six little feet in a marche militaire.

In other poems I have not been overly literal but ever aware of what Campana is saying. The word *muto* may be rendered mute, dumb, speechless:

> Al giardino spettrale al lauro muto
> To the spectral garden to the silenced laurel.

I preferred *silenced* since birdsong no longer redeemed the tree in the autumnal garden.

★

This letter, submitted with the poem, "The Chimera" to the editor of *La Voce* was never answered:

Distinguished Mr. Prezzolini,

I address myself to you, eminent Sir. I am a poor devil who writes as he feels: perhaps you will be willing to listen. I am that specimen who was introduced to you by Mr. Soffici at the Futurist Exhibition as a misfit, a so-and-so who from time to time writes something worthwhile. I write prose poems and poetry: no one wants to publish me and I need to be published; in order to prove to myself I exist and to keep on writing I need to be published. I add that I deserve to be published since I feel that that bit of

poetry I know how to create has a purity of accent that is little common among us today. I am not ambitious but I think that after having been tossed about the world and mangled by life, my word despite its wit has a right to be heard. However little I know you I am certain you have a sensitive soul which feels the justice of my appeal as you will the truth in my poetry. I am certain you are not a part of the ironic gang of frauds. I prefer to send you my oldest and frankest poems, old in metaphor yet intricate in form; however you will hear a spirit that frees itself — I wait in complete trust — in homage I revere you.

Dino Campana
Marradi, 6 January 1914

NOTES ON THE TEXT

INTRODUCTION

Orphic Songs: The Orphic mysteries, dating from the 6th century B.C., embodied the esoteric doctrines and rites practiced by worshipers of Dionysus, the bull god, claiming Orpheus as their founder. Their central doctrine was the immortality of the soul. Reborn after death, the initiate was transported to the Islands of the Blessed. The tenets of Orphism are inscribed on eight golden funerary tablets, seven unearthed in Italy and one in Crete. Orphic hymns, a body of songs in praise of the gods, have not survived, but imitations, the Alexandrian forgeries, dating from the 4th century A.D., are extant.

Walt Whitman: In Stanza 34 of "Song of Myself," Whitman tells of "the glory of the race of rangers" massacred at the Alamo.

> None obey'd the command to kneel
>
> . . . .
>
> A youth not seventeen years old seiz'd his assassin till
>   two more came to release him;
> The three were all torn, and cover'd with the boy's blood.

La Voce: Ardengo Soffici (1879–1964), Giovanni Papini (1881–1956), and Giuseppe Prezzolini (1882–   ) declared themselves as "pagan in religion and individualists in life." It was the war and its aftermath that turned Papini back to the church and Soffici into an insufferable patriot. Prezzolini became a distinguished Professor of Italian at Columbia University.

Autumnal Garden: There are correspondences between this poem and its variant *Boboli*. *A piercing fanfare is heard/rising* is the

trumpet call from the armory in Boboli Garden at the Pitti Palace in Florence.

The Glass Window: In Marradi the Little Madonna in a framed niche on the wall overlooked the bridge, bombed out by the Americans during World War II. Today there is a Little Madonna in her niche on the wall upstreet from the new bridge.

Metaphors for a Journey and a Mountain: In line two *the more powerful second soul* is the substance in which the spirit, or first soul, is submerged. Substance overwhelms every timidity in the flesh and realizes its power.

Journey to Montevideo: The equatorial city is Capoverde. The wild shore is the Uruguayan coast. The marine capital is Buenos Aires.

Fantasy on a Painting by Ardengo Soffici: Opposed to the Futurist doctrines of Soffici, Campana has written a poem not as way out as Marinetti but in keeping with the concept of the Futurists.

Dualism: Manuelita Etchegarray is the name attributed to a girl in Bahia Blanca, a seaport 350 miles southwest of Buenos Aires.

Dream in Prison: Whoever Anika may be, Campana remembers her in this pastiche recalling his imprisonment in Belgium.

Genoa: There is a provocative ambiguity in the repeated use of *alto sale* (salty height) and the verb *salì* (it arose). The infinitive *salire* has for its third person singular in the present tense the verb *sale*, its spelling identical with the noun *sale* (salt). Ramat, editor of the current Italian edition of *Canti Orfici*, agrees with this interpretation.

La Superba is an epithet for Genoa.

Ship on its Way: Under the editorship of De Robertis, this lyric appeared in "La Voce" following the publication of *Orphic Songs.*

Oscar Wilde at San Miniato: The basilica, closed in by cypresses, stands on a hill overlooking Florence. Campana was eleven years old at the time of Wilde's death. The title is enigmatic.

182

Fatuous Florence: Every day a cannon announced the noon hour.

Old Florence: In the embrasures of the Palazzo Vecchio oil pots are lit on festive or on holy evenings.

Boboli: See Autumnal Garden above.

The Creation: Except for one accidental comma, this poem is written without punctuation.

Trembling of Tombs: This poem has its counterpart in *Enormous Tomb of the Sea.*

In the Thundering Twilight has the tone, quality, and substance of Genoa.

Blonde Ceres: The four poems in this group are dedicated to Sibilla Aleramo, the Millay of Italy, with whom Campana had a whirlwind love affair. The third lyric is unique in Italian love poetry: "We made the roses fade that were not our roses/My roses her roses / P.S. And so we forgot the roses.

Franco-Italian Proletarian Song: The red jacket of the stars is a Campanesque conceit that has its metaphoric origin in *Giubbe Rosse (Red Jackets),* the café in the Piazza della Repùbblica.

Biology: Monsieur Pappin is a derogatory allusion to Papini, whose pedestrian verses Campana could not abide.

Prospectus III: Giovanni Giolitti, who was five-time president of the Consiglio, and energetically conducted the war against Libya as he energetically fought for universal suffrage, is the object of this satirical allegory. In 1914 he wanted Italy to be neutral, much to the discomfiture of the military. Here Campana has Italy walk "with the tread of a Nietzschean beast among the mythological vegetables."

Observations: I (No. 16): Campana, as a Tuscan-Romagnan, has an antipathy to Gentile and Croce, southerners, no matter how valid their philosophies. When he says he "arrived . . . at the logic of Louvain," he refers to Cardinal Mercier, the Neo-Scholastic.